THE P(

STAR

METHOD

HOW TO SUCCEED AT BEHAVIORAL JOB INTERVIEW

Martha Gage
2022

Images: Freepik.com/storyset

ISBN: 979-8848463293

Your Bonus is Here!

Dear Reader,

As a way of saying thanks for your purchase, I'm offering the *"STAR Interview Practice Worksheet"*, alongside a set of valuable resource lists. These extras are a great complementary addition to this guide and will be very helpful in your preparation process.

Download these extras by scanning the QR-code below

Table of Contents

Introduction

The road to having a job always truly begins with an interview. You have to impress the interviewer enough during the interview to start every new job. But what is an interview and what value does it hold?

An interview is a face-to-face conversation between the interviewer and the interviewee, where the interviewer seeks answers from the interviewee for choosing a potential new employee.

The interview is the most critical component of the entire selection process. It serves as the primary means of collecting additional information about an applicant, as the basis for assessing an applicant's job-related knowledge, skills, and abilities. It is designed to decide if an individual should be interviewed further, hired, or eliminated from consideration.

Interviewers use many different types of interviews to evaluate interviewees. One of these types, called behavioral interviewing, has recently risen to become the world's most widely used approach.In a behavioral interview, the candidate provides concrete examples about how they used specific behaviors or skills on the job. A candidate's answers help the interviewer get an accurate picture of not only what the candidate can do, but also how they do it. In order to present an answer in the most effective way, interviewees should use the so-called STAR method for responses, which this guide is all about.

Preparing for your interviews with this book will allow you to gain confidence as you gain knowledge. The most successful candidates get more job offers by delivering the information the interviewer is looking for with confidence. *The Power of STAR Method* will make your interviewing more meaningful and successful!

Purpose of this Guide

This comprehensive guide offers an effective way for you to handle behavioral interviews so that you will emphasize the knowledge, skills, and abilities that you have, and that employers demand.

The purpose of this guide is to provide you with all the necessary information, such as:

- common types of behavioral questions
- strategy for handling behavioral interviews
- detailed step-by-step instructions on preparing for the STAR interview (research, predicting possible questions, developing your stories, etc.)
- 20 most common behavioral questions, the mindset behind asking them, and advice on how to prepare winning answers to these questions
- the most common mistakes to avoid
- tips to show the best of your personality

- STAR resume and cover letter as a way to increase chance of invitation to interview

And much more.

This book may very well be your first stepping stone toward growth in your career. If you master the art of STAR response, you can win any job and take a step closer to your dream!

CHAPTER 1

What is Behavioral Interview and Why is it Important?

The interview itself is an important step in the process of selecting potential new employees and even the planning of promotions. Interviews can offer benefits to the organizing bodies that use them, including:

- being a starting opportunity for employers to meet the job candidates.
- giving time for people, such as those in HR and hiring managers, among others, to meet with candidates to get a feel for traits or qualities and behaviors that can't be found in applications, resumes, or even recommendations.
- allowing the employer to see if a candidate's traits meet the job requirements.
- aiding the employer to determine if an applicant will be able to fit into the workplace culture.

The technique that many consider to be the most effective is *behavioral interviewing*; this interviewing technique focuses on the past experiences of the candidate being interviewed. It is done by asking candidates to give specific examples of how they have previously demonstrated their particular traits. The answers to the questions should provide evidence of the candidate's suitability that should be able to be verified. The information provided often reveals to the employer the actual level of experience and ability to handle possible situations in the future that might be similar. These types of questions tend to be blunt, probing, and specific.

In addition, the behavioral method of interviewing falls under the category of *structured interviews*. The main point of structural interviewing is to match and compare candidates for positions by asking questions that are related to the job and using predetermined ratings to evaluate them in an objective manner. Approaching an interview this way limits the amount of potential bias on the side of the individual interviewer and makes it easier to compare applicants in a fair manner, because all applicants are asked the same questions and evaluated using the same criteria. In short, structured interviewing isn't just effective for helping to make a hiring decision, it might be crucial to defending against possible allegations of discrimination in selection and hiring.

However, there are additional benefits to using behavioral interviews. As they are based around analyzing the duties and requirements of a job, there is a reduction in bias and ambiguity as candidates are evaluated on questions related to the job. Also, consistency and relativity of the interview process to the job might increase the perception of fairness among the candidates. These job-related questions might even help candidates gain a realistic perspective of the job they are applying for.

The basis for behavioral interviewing is that past performances in similar situations is the most accurate predictor of future performances. To determine it more fairly and effectively, the main questions that are given to every candidate are worded the same way in the same order and using the same scoring system. According to Katharine Hansen, Ph.D., Creative Director and Associate Publisher of Quintessential Careers, behavioral interviewing is said to be 55% predictive of future job behavior compared to traditional interviewing, which is only 10% predictive.

In traditional interviews, questions that have straightforward answers are asked, such as *"What are your strengths and weaknesses?"*

It is important to understand the differences between behavioral and situational interview questions. The former type of questions ask candidates to share specific situations when they've had to use certain skills, or to explain how they've handled certain types of scenarios. Behavioral questions typically start with, *"Tell me about a time when..."* The latter are more theoretical explorations of how you might act in a future situation; they typically begin with, *"How would you act if..."*

Behavioral interviewing is said to provide more objective sets of facts to make employment decisions compared to other interviewing methods.

CHAPTER 2

What the Interviewer Really Wants to Know

The behavioral interview technique is used by employers to determine an applicant's chance for success based on their experiences and behaviors. The interviewer identifies the job-related traits that the company has deemed to be desirable to their positions. Interviewers typically compile behavioral questions in two categories:

1. **Job function.** This means the key traits that are necessary for performing the role successfully; referring to the abilities, knowledge, and skills that the position requires.

2. **Culture and values.** Because each company has a unique culture, it is always worthwhile to ask candidates behavioral questions that will tell you if they will be able to thrive in your workplace.

Behavioral interviewing is essentially lending itself to an approach that is based on competencies to identify the job requirements. There are specific employee behaviors that relate to a company's strategic goals. Job performance can be measured across multiple business systems to improve the company's overall performance; these are called *competencies*.

There are many benefits to using an approach based on competencies in behavioral interviewing:

- **They provide direction.** Competencies give companies a way to define, in behavioral terms, what it is that potential candidates need to do in order to produce the results that the company wants, in a way that aligns with its culture.

- **They are measurable.** Competencies let companies evaluate the extent to which candidates demonstrate the kinds of behaviors that are crucial for success and for strengthening the company's ability to reach their strategic objectives.

- **They can be learned.** Competencies are characteristics that can be developed and improved, unlike personality traits.

- **They can distinguish the company.** Competencies are representative of the values with which a company distinguishes itself.

By using competencies in interviewing, employers can glean important information as to whether or not a candidate is capable of performing all the necessary job requirements while being a good fit for the company.

When interviewers ask a potential new hire a behavioral question, the interviewee is expected to give an answer that provides information in the form of a short story. However, when telling the story, they can't just breeze through talking about the activities and tasks that were accomplished; they are expected to talk about how they accomplished them. It is up to the interviewer to encourage the interviewee to give the details of their achievements, their response to challenges, and the ways in which they differentiate themselves from other employees, so they can collect evidence of their fitness for the job. In the case of examples based in team settings, the candidates should answer these questions in a way that highlights what they did as individuals, using the word "I" and not "we."

When questions begin with one of the following examples below, it is a sign that it is a behavioral question:

- *Tell me about a time when...*
- *Have you ever...*
- *Give me an example of...*
- *Describe when you...*
- *What do you do when...*

Interviewers prefer these questions because it helps them to get a good sense of how you behave and work.

In addition, it helps them to see what you're capable of accomplishing by examining your past work performance. Look at it from the interviewer's perspective: Would you be more convinced of someone's ability to work on a team by them simply saying that they love working on a team, or by them telling a story that demonstrates exactly how they work with a team to overcome a difficult obstacle?

CHAPTER 3

Common Types of Competency-Based Questions

Interviewers might ask a variety of questions regarding competencies that depend on the skills necessary for a specific job. Unfortunately, there isn't a way to predict the exact list of questions that you'll be asked; but, the good news is that these behavioral questions tend to be related to common themes. Outlined below are some of the popular themes, including a few sample behavioral questions for each. The exact wording may be different during the actual interview, but the themes the interviewer is interested in will likely be the same.

Leadership

Leadership qualities aren't just for management positions; hiring managers look for leadership abilities at all levels, as the skills show potential for future growth. Examples include being able to mentor or train others, decision-making, problem solving, and taking initiative. Leadership is about stepping out there and showing others the way, as well as connecting with everyone else and forging a path together.

Sample Questions:

- *Tell me about someone you have personally mentored.*
- *Describe a time when you had to make an unpopular decision.*
- *Describe a time when you showed initiative and caused others to follow.*

Teamwork

Teamwork is crucial to a company's ability to make ongoing profits. When employees work together, they grow together, and issues rarely arise that can't be handled with the cooperation of people with a range of skills. The hiring managers will be on the lookout for your ability to communicate effectively and work through challenges with other people. As you are telling your stories, they will also be looking for clues to understand what kind of role you will take in a team environment.

Sample Questions:

- *What role do you assume when you work within a team?*
- *Describe a time when you disagreed with a team member. How did you resolve the problem?*
- *Tell me about a time you needed to get information from someone who wasn't very responsive. What did you do?*

Problem Solving

Problems are a normal part of life, and work is no exception. Hiring managers will want to know about your resourcefulness: your ability to analyze any situation, to find solutions, and to follow through on them. Think about a few problems that you've solved successfully and be prepared to share them.

Sample Questions:

- *Tell me about a time when you improved a process or made something more efficient.*

- *Tell me about the last customer issue you were tasked with.*
- *Tell me about a time when you used creativity to overcome a dilemma.*

Conflict Resolution

We live in a world of competing priorities and heated opinions, so conflict is never too far away. A lot of companies look to foster healthy competition as a strategy to achieve great results. Conflicts and disagreements are a part of life, which means that hiring managers are interested in seeing how you handle difficult situations. The negative ones can be hard to talk about, but you should keep your stories as positive as possible; just focus on what happened, what the resolution was, and what you learned from the incidents. Your answers should show the interviewer that you're able to manage conflict in a professional manner.

Sample Questions:

- *Tell me about a time when you had to deal with an angry or dissatisfied customer.*
- *Have you ever had to mediate a conflict between two colleagues?*
- *Tell me about a time when you have worked with others who thought differently.*

Communication

Effective communication is vital to a working environment, whether it is explaining processes, building relationships, sharing ideas, or setting expectations. If we are able to get our messages across to other parties, whether spoken or written, we have a chance of discovering like-minded collaborators and influential sponsors; we achieve nothing if there isn't any communication.

Sample Questions:

- *Give me an example of a time when you were able to successfully persuade someone at work to see things your way.*

- *Tell me about a successful presentation you gave and why you think it was a hit.*
- *Describe a time in your career when you had to say "no" to a colleague.*

Adaptability

In cases where there are multiple ways to solve a problem, the most flexible and innovative approach will win out. You need to be adaptable, as you never know what life might throw at you next; when you are in a business environment that is fast-changing, adaptability means having the ability to change when a situation demands it. Explain to your interviewer how you've adapted to a new communication or working style, navigated through previously uncharted territory, and how you reacted to unpredictable situations. The key words you need to think about when answering are: improvise, adapt, and overcome.

Sample Questions:

- *Give me an example of a time when you had to think on your feet.*
- *Tell me about a time you failed. How did you deal with the situation?*
- *Describe a time when you had to do something outside your scope of work.*

Stress Management

When it comes to an effective workplace, the importance of mental health should never be underestimated. If your mind is imbalanced your work can be disrupted, and everything will seem much more difficult than usual. Learning to manage not just your own stress, but also the stress of those around you, is a pressure-release valve that can be activated when times get tough. When giving examples, stick to the ones where you kept your cool when the situation got stressful; you should also give evidence of how you handled your stress and reduced its effects.

19

Sample Questions:

- *Tell me about a time when you felt that you couldn't cope.*
- *Share a time when you had to complete a project without the required resources.*
- *Give an example of when you faced a stressful situation. How did you approach it?*

Time Management

Time is a resource that runs out, and it can easily pass us by or be wasted through mindless chatting or completing unimportant tasks. To be a good time manager at work you have to be disciplined and mindful of the exact ways you can move a step or two closer to your goals. You have to give priority to what is important and to keep everyone and everything moving along. When your interviewer asks about your time management skills, be prepared to talk about specific times when you had a few things to be done and how you prioritized, scheduled, organized, and completed them all, preferably before a deadline.

Sample Questions:

- *Tell me about a time when you had to handle your routine being disrupted?*
- *Describe a time when it was clear that you wouldn't meet a deadline.*
- *Describe a long-term project that you kept on track. How did you keep everything moving?*

Decision Making

Endless possibilities are a factor of life, so having the ability to make informed decisions can mean the difference between success and failure. How you make those decisions will be of interest to your future employer, so prepare a few stories that highlight how you balance risk and rewards for an interesting addition to your career history. Don't forget to talk about having made logical and well-thought-out decisions, as well as your critical thinking skills;

remember also to discuss your decision process and not the results alone.

Sample Questions:

- *Describe a situation when you had to make a decision with insufficient data.*
- *Give me an example of a time you had to make a tough decision.*
- *Could you tell me about when you covered your teammate and needed to make decisions on their behalf?*

Goal Orientation

Those who set the highest ambitions don't always get there, but they can achieve far more than the average person who is happy with the mundane. Setting and resetting your goals as you progress in your career is a great way to ensure your professional growth; not many employers want an employee who is content with sitting still.

Sample Questions:

- *Tell me about an occasion when you failed to do what you had promised.*
- *Share a time when you went above and beyond what was expected of you.*
- *Tell me about a time when you had to align your colleagues behind your ideas.*

While the main competencies have been described in this chapter, this isn't a complete list, as there are also competencies like personal development, work ethic, attitude toward failures, customer service, motivation, values, etc. You can find sample questions for them in the additional materials to this book (see *"400+ Popular Competency Based Behavioral Interview Questions"* sheet).

CHAPTER 4

Strategy for Handling Behavioral Interviews

There's no doubt that, for those being interviewed, behavioral interview questions are one of the biggest sore spots, as the interviewer isn't just looking for simple yes or no answers; they are looking for short, yet somewhat detailed stories.

That also applies to applicants who don't have work experience; in those cases, behavioral questions and answers can be based on other situations that you've encountered, such as volunteering responsibilities or university projects.

While the goal of the interviewer is to learn more about you, you too have a goal, which is to present yourself in the best possible way. To do that, there are a few things to do before every interview:

1. Spend time researching

Research the company. Learn as much as you can about your prospective employer before you go in for your interview. Look over the company website and pay attention to their history, mission statement, and anything else that pertains to their corporate values. Follow the company on social media, paying attention to how they present their company culture; look up their profile on *LinkedIn* and read their employee reviews on *Glassdoor.*

Research the job description. Give yourself time to really look over the job description and highlight the experience and skills that are required for you to succeed in the role. Once you've carefully reviewed the job listing, write down all abilities and skills needed for the position. Examples can include collaboration, leadership, problem-solving, attention to detail, presentation skills, etc.

Research the interviewer. If you know the name of the hiring manager before you meet with them, take a look at their LinkedIn profile and social media presence. However, the goal here is not to force a connection, but to look for similarities in your background, career goals, and interests that may help you connect with them during the interview.

2. Create a list of example situations

In order to be well prepared for the interview, after you've done the research listed above, think about situations that you've dealt with that demonstrate the skills and qualities that the interviewer is looking for. If you are new to the workforce and don't have a job history to draw from, consider using volunteer, schooling, or internship experiences, if you have them. Sometimes, interviewers might even ask you to share non-work examples, so you should think about challenges and obstacles that you've overcome in your personal life too.

3. Transform example situations into STAR stories

But, the most important part of answering behavioral questions is their organization and structure; every response must follow the STAR format. Take your list of situations and use them to prepare an answer for each question using this format. This will help give you a response that is brief, coherent, and structured to the questions. The STAR method is dealt with in more detail in *Chapter 6*.

4. Practice talking through your answers out loud

One of the most effective ways to prepare for a job interview is to practice saying your answers out loud; repeat them a few times, but there's no need to memorize your responses. You can even do this in front of a mirror in order to get a better sense of how you are presenting yourself as you answer. The more comfortable you are voicing your answers, the more natural you will sound when the interview comes.

Being successful during an interview is all about preparation; there aren't necessarily any wrong answers. These kinds of questions are geared toward your interviewer getting to know the real you; what is important is that you are honest and that you structure your answers in a way that communicates what you have to offer.

Strategy for Handling Behavioral Interviews

Spend time researching	⇨	Create a list of example situations	⇨	Transform them into STAR stories	⇨	Practice saying your answers out loud

Research the company

Research the job description

Research the interviewer

CHAPTER 5

What is the STAR Interview Method?

Star Framework

The STAR interview method consists of four key parts, and provides a framework for how to respond to behavioral interview questions. These types of questions can cause interviewees to feel the urge to ramble on, but using the STAR method helps to keep answers short and to the point.

The four parts are described in detail below:

Situation: *What was going on?*

Set up the story by sharing with the interviewer the context surrounding the challenge or situation that you faced. In the majority of cases, it is best to describe relevant work situations, but it might also be a good idea to talk about academic projects or volunteer work, depending on the amount of transferable experience you have. It is also important to talk about specific circumstances rather than general responsibilities.

However, this is the part that you should spend the least amount of time talking about, as the interviewers prefer to know more about the actions that you took and what the results of those actions were.

Tip: Just share enough detail to provide context to the situation: when it was, who was there, where it happened, and how the situation came to this point.

Example: *"In my previous job as an advertising executive, one of my coworkers quit immediately after signing the biggest client the firm had ever landed."*

Task: *What was your goal?*

Describe your role or responsibility in the challenge or situation. basically talk about the goal or task that had been set out for you. This part doesn't require a lot of detail, either; stick to one or two points that illustrate the task that needed completion.

Tip: Your interviewer is more likely to want to hear about measurable things, so include details such as beating a deadline, or the size of an order. It is also good to talk about any kind of constraint or special issue you had to face.

Example: *"Although I was already managing a full load of accounts, I was assigned this new client as well. I knew that the stakes were high and that we wouldn't hit our quarterly goal if we lost this deal."*

Action: *What did you do?*

Talk about the specific actions that you undertook to overcome the challenge or handle the situation. This is the part of your answer that requires the most in-depth description, because it is what largely indicates how much potential you have for fitting a role. Identify and discuss a few of the important steps you took that gained you success.

For the most part, challenges in the workplace are solved by a team; but, it is a common downfall to use "we"' when describing how you achieved your goals during an interview. Instead, focus on what you did in the situation; it can be helpful to remember that the interviewer's intention is to hire you and you alone for a job, so you should be using "I" to showcase your contributions.

Tip: Focus on describing your own actions; you don't want to make the interviewer feel like they should be hiring someone else on your team.

Example: *"I first took some time to lower my stress levels, then I carefully gauged and reorganized my task list to ensure that I would be able to manage all my duties. Thanks to these actions, and by giving up a few evenings and weekends, I was able to be completely available to the client and complete the project on time."*

Result: *What was the outcome?*

What outcome was reached as a result of your actions? This is an important part of your response to focus on; you should spend only somewhat less time discussing your results compared to talking about your actions. Choose two or three of your most impressive results and talk about those.

Show off your success or give solid examples of the positive effects of your efforts. You should also discuss what you learned, how you grew, and why you are a stronger employee because of the experience.

Tip: The interviewer wants to hear about results that are specific and measurable, so don't make the common mistake of talking about results that you simply feel were positive.

Example: *"The client was so impressed with my dedication to their satisfaction that they immediately signed an annual contract that earned my company $4 million."*

Situation	Task	Action	Result
What was going on?	What was your goal?	What did you do?	What was the outcome?

The STAR structure is easy to remember, simple to follow, and offers great responses that should satisfy all but the most curious interviewers; although, if they do want to ask follow-up questions to clarify aspects of your story, that's always an option.

The STAR method does not work well if you're trying to do some "truth-stretching" and exaggerate your accomplishments beyond putting your behavior in a favorable light. Naturally, what is a downside for weak candidates is an upside for strong candidates.

Star Alternatives

The advantage of using a structure like STAR is that it's logical and it makes it easy to remember the parts to include in your responses to interview questions. However, STAR is not the only method available. Below are some examples of alternatives:

- PAR (Problem, Action, Result)
- SAR (Situation, Action, Result)
- SOAR (Situation, Obstacle, Action, Result)
- CAR (Context/Challenge, Action, Result)
- EAR (Example, Action, Result)

The techniques noted above are very similar to the STAR method; the difference is that the majority of them are 3-step methods compared to the 4-step method of STAR. The first letter in these acronyms typically combines the S and T steps, which is an ideal strategy to briefly describe the situation. Words like Problem, Context, and Example are similar to the Situation and Task of STAR; so the basic method remains the same.

CHAPTER 6

STAR Interview Preparation Process in Detail

Compared to technical interviews, the preparation needed for a behavioral interview takes less time; on average, it takes only one or two hours over three to four days to get comfortable with the interview process, example questions, and personalized stories.

But how do you go about preparing for your interview? Where do you start? What questions do you go over? The truth is that there are certain types of behavioral questions that are asked more often than others; a total of seven categories can be identified. From knowing these common types of questions, you can prepare a successful story for each category and show off your skills.

The seven must-have story categories are:

1. **Leadership:** A story of when you became a leader and took charge.

2. **Teamwork:** A story of when you cooperated on a team and helped others.

3. Problem-Solving: A story of when you solved a big problem and/or overcame a big challenge or obstacle.

4. Achievement: A story of when you achieved something great and/or something that you're proud of.

5. Work Ethic: A story of when you went above and beyond.

6. Conflict Resolution: A story of when you worked with a difficult colleague or customer and how you handled it.

7. Failure: A story of when you failed or messed up and what you learned from it.

In addition, you should also develop other types of stories that are related to your field and which highlight the attributes, skills, and values that are most important for the job or program you're applying for. To figure out these extra categories or competencies, you should do initial research of the job description ahead of time.

The process gets simpler and more organized by following the six steps listed below.

Step 1: Gathering Required Abilities and Skills

The first thing to do is to research competencies that are required for the job position, as behavioral questions can be based on a wide variety of them. Do review the job description and keep an eye out for keywords and phrases, or necessary skills that are included.

The interviewers will tailor their behavioral questions to determine if you are the right fit for the job; which will, of course, reflect the duties, qualifications, and responsibilities that are listed in the description. Through reading the job description repeatedly, you can eventually predict what behavioral questions the interviewer might ask you. For example, if you are being interviewed for a position that requires good time management, you might be asked something like, *"Tell me about a time that you had to navigate your schedule around a full workload; how did you overcome it?"*

It will help you to carefully pick out noticeable key words and phrases from the job description to discover any specific competencies mentioned outside of the seven most common ones, as well as to make possible predictions of behavioral questions and create concise and relevant answers to them.

Step 2: Brainstorming Related Experience

Identifying your related past experience will help you come up with relevant examples to give your interviewer. Using the list below as inspiration, make a list of the specific jobs, classes, etc. that helped you to gain experience.

- Attended a conference or other event
- College major, minor, or other classes
- Research or other projects
- Shadowing or observation experience
- Similar role in a previous position (even if it was in a different field)
- Skills and abilities

- Trainings or certifications
- Volunteer experience in the field
- Work or internship experience in field

Make sure to note down every organization that you were a part of, such as academics, clubs, internships, societies, etc.

Step 3: Brainstorming Examples

Your next step is to brainstorm the specific examples that you will use for your answers. Think of the related experiences that you identified in Step 2 and write down two to three ideas for each of the seven common categories. Next, take that list of skills that you created and find those qualities that the company is looking for in a candidate; they should be clearly stated in the job description. Use the guiding questions below to help you brainstorm examples of situations that demonstrate your competency in each of these common categories:

Leadership: *Can you think of a time when you had to take charge of a group? Can you tell of a time where you had to prove yourself a good team leader? Have you ever had to motivate a team during a difficult time?*

Teamwork: *Can you give an example where you were on a team that had to really pull together to complete an assignment or project? How do you feel about being on a team? Have you ever had difficulties working on a team?*

Problem-Solving: *Can you think of a time when things didn't go as planned but worked out in the end? How did you handle an upset client/customer? How did you get past a late shipment?*

Achievement: *What is the hardest project you've ever done for work? Have you ever received an award or honors? When have you done your best work?*

Work Ethic: *Can you think of a time when you really wanted to give a project your all? Are you willing to work overtime? Have you ever* *had to go an extra mile to complete a project?*

Conflict Resolution: *Can you think of a time when you had to sit down with a classmate or coworker to settle a disagreement? Have you ever felt nervous to discuss something with a coworker or supervisor but were relieved after finally talking to them? How did you express your opposition to something and how did it turn out?*

Failure: *What's something that you would do differently now if you had the chance? What is a time where you failed at a deadline? What is your worst failure?*

Step 4: Choosing Quality Examples

Now we'll take a closer look and decide which examples to use for your interview; it is important to pick the ones that best demonstrate that you are qualified for the position. Take the list that you brainstormed in Step 3 and go through the checklist below.

CIRCLE any examples of:

- related experiences that you identified in Step 2
- calculable results, including the number of customers, the amount of money, etc.
- positive outcomes, when everything worked out great in the end
- stories that you enjoy telling
- stories that you would feel comfortable telling to someone who looks up to you
- stories that would make you want to hire someone if you were the interviewer

CROSS OUT any examples of:

- situations that are more personal than professional
- high school experiences, if you are 21 or older; high-school examples are okay if you are under 21, but prioritize college examples if available
- situations with a negative outcome

- situations that upset you, like anger towards a boss or classmate
- stories that you wouldn't tell to people whose opinion you value
- stories that wouldn't make you want to hire someone if you were the interviewer

Now, from your list of good examples, choose at least one that relates to each of the competency categories.

Step 5: Writing Your STAR Stories

Transforming Your Situation Into Story

Describe your chosen situations in detail in accordance with the STAR method, writing two or three sentences for each of the four categories. We'll break it down using the following behavioral question as an example:

"Tell me about a time that you made a mistake, but learned from it."

Situation: Explain your story's context; don't forget to include the who, what, where, when, and how.

"There was a time during my previous employment when I was learning a new software in my field that I was unfamiliar with and it was a requirement for the job to learn it. Once my training was complete, I was instructed to take on a simple workload that took two days; however, I was informed afterward that I had made several errors."

Task: What were you asked to do? What was the end game? Explain the task you had to complete while highlighting any specific challenges or constraints such as costs, deadlines, or other issues.

"I was instructed to correct my mistakes and was given a small window of half a work day to turn it in."

Action: Outline the steps that you took to solve the problem. What actions did you take? Try to match up your actions to the job requirements.

35

"I walked myself through my training with the new software to identify where I had made my errors. It was through this process that I successfully discovered where I had gone wrong."

Result: Use this to share the outcome. What was the end result of your work? How was the situation resolved? You need to be as specific as possible and share measurable numbers when you can.

"I was able to finish my corrections within the time allotted to me, and at the same time I had retrained myself in the software and learned to never make the same mistakes again."

Following the STAR method will help you give the kinds of detailed responses that the interviewer will expect when they are asking a behavioral-based interview question. It isn't too difficult to do, either; as long as you work out each of the steps in the STAR method in order, you'll hit your answer and impress your interviewer at the same time.

Enriching Your Story With Powerful Words

The kinds of words that you use during an interview can make a difference; think about the difference between these two responses:

- *"I helped brainstorm ideas for marketing."*
- *"I generated great ideas that were used in many successful advertising campaigns."*

Both of the answers are reasonable, but one of them shows significant accomplishments and makes a stronger positive impression while the other response is bland and easy to forget.

Let's delve deeper to see why the second response is more powerful compared to the first one. To begin with, the word "helped" from the first response is too vague; from the interviewer's point of view, it could mean that you presented some original ideas, but it could also mean that you were an almost silent participant on a conference call to discuss the project. On the other hand, the second option contains a more active verb, as a person who generates ideas is someone who is deeply involved with a project. Also, a more powerful adjective is added; not only did you come up with ideas, but they were great ones! However, you need to be careful not to overuse adjectives in your speech; those are more suited to your resume.

So, no doubt you've noticed that it is crucial to include powerful words in your story; powerful words can come in the form of action verbs (e.g. demonstrate, evaluate, etc.), adjectives (e.g. focused, respectful, etc.) or nouns, when naming soft skills (e.g. assertiveness, motivation, etc.). Active language can make or break your story, and adding a little spice to it by using strong words is an excellent way to enhance its delivery.

But, you might wonder, where does one find these kinds of words?

Firstly, you can again use the list of research results that you created in Step 1 and patch your answers with keywords that are appropriate to the situation.

Secondly, this book contains additional material in later chapters, where you will be shown the most common examples of powerful words to use in your stories, as well as extended lists of action verbs, adjectives, and soft skills for different categories (e.g. communication, leadership, responsibility, etc.).

Useful Sentence Starters

Below are some useful ways to start off your sentences for each part of the STAR method that will help signal to your interviewers that you are using this method.

Situation
- *In my last/previous role as...*
- *During a project on...*
- *While working on...*

Task
- *My supervisor asked me to...*
- *My task was...*

- *I was responsible for...*
- *I was in charge of...*
- *It was my role to...*

Action

- *I provided...*
- *I organized...*
- *I developed...*
- *I conducted...*
- *I mediated...*

Result

- *By doing [x] I was able to...*
- *As a result...*
- *This allowed my team/department to...*
- *I achieved...*
- *I advanced...*
- *I learnt...*

STAR Technique Templates

Below are some answer templates that might be useful to you.

STAR technique template #1:

Situation: *In my previous role as a **[job title]**, there was **[describe your problem]**.*

Task: *My job was **[your responsibilities]**.*

Action: *I needed to **[list out the actions taken to resolve the problem]**.*

Result: *In the end, I achieved **[outcome #1]** and **[outcome #2]**.*

STAR technique template #2:

Situation: *During my previous employment, I was a **[job title]**. My role was to **[job tasks and responsibilities]**.*

Task: *The goal was to **[expected outcome]**.*

Action: In order to achieve these results, I [describe what you have done in detail]. I utilized the skills I learned such as *[hard skill #1]* and *[hard skill #2]* in addition to my comprehensive understanding of *[your area of specialization].*

Result: In the end, I achieved [achievement #1] and [achievement #2].

STAR technique template #3:

Situation: During [the specific time/period], I needed to [explain the situation].

Task: I felt [how it affected you].

Action: I attempted to [what you have done to cope with it].

Result: In the end, I was able to [accomplishment #1], and [accomplishment #2].

STAR technique template #4:

Situation: While working on [specific project], [details about problem/challenge].

Task: I was in charge of [specific responsibilities].

Action: I provided [specific details].

Result: I helped achieve [achievement #1] and [achievement #2].

STAR technique template #5:

Situation: During a project on [specific subject], [explain the situation].

Task: It was my role to [specific details].

Action: I organized [specific details].

Result: This allowed my team/department to [outcome #1] and [outcome #2].

Step 6: Practice

You now have brainstormed your related experiences, identified your best examples, and written your stories using the STAR method. You have done a lot of work to get ready for your interview, and now you will be prepared, professional, and convincing when you walk into that room. But there is still one step left, and that is practicing your stories so you can deliver them with clarity and confidence. Below is a list of ways you can practice; for best results, complete the entire list.

- After completing Step 5, take a day or two to sleep on it, then re-read all of your stories and revise any parts that you think need improvement. Then, re-write your revised stories on a new piece of paper.

- Say the stories aloud to yourself in front of a mirror; don't memorize your answers, simply say them a few times.

- Look over the list of possible questions in the additional material of this book (see *"400+ Popular Competency Based Behavioral Interview Questions"* sheet). This will help with anticipating possible questions, so you can adapt the wording of your answers a little; trying out different ways of telling the same story can help make it sound natural.

- Use your phone to record yourself telling your stories and then listen to them. See if you notice whether or not you sound confident and positive, speak clearly, etc. Then record yourself again.

- Ask a trusted family member or friend to listen and ask for feedback and suggestions. Pick someone that you think is a professional and has been successful with their own interviews.

In the additional materials to this book, you will find the *"STAR Interview Practice Worksheet"*, which will guide you through all steps mentioned above. Just download it, print it and start developing your stories.

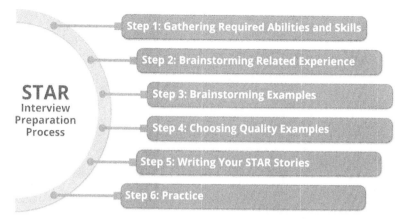

STAR
Interview
Preparation
Process

Step 1: Gathering Required Abilities and Skills

Step 2: Brainstorming Related Experience

Step 3: Brainstorming Examples

Step 4: Choosing Quality Examples

Step 5: Writing Your STAR Stories

Step 6: Practice

CHAPTER 7

Powerful Words to Use in an Interview

As nerve-wracking as they are, the advantage of having job interviews is that they give you the opportunity to impress the people who might hire you, and to prove your abilities, skills, and qualifications are on par with what is required for the position. Being able to communicate your personality and skills in a proper and professional manner while using strong words is important to make sure that the interviewer clearly understands what you have to offer. Interviews are meant to be conversations in which the interviewer and applicant decide if the latter is suitable for the position and company culture. When you speak in a way that demonstrates professionalism and portrays your abilities and qualifications, in addition to asking specific questions, it can be a positive influence on the interviewer's perception of you. Using the kinds of words that are aspirational and positive during your interview can further demonstrate your confidence and professionalism as well as your own beliefs about your abilities to perform well on the job.

In this chapter we explore the importance of using powerful words during a job interview while providing several examples of words that you can use in your next interview to help stand out from the other applicants. Below are eight broad types of words and phrases to integrate with your answers.

Communication

Being able to communicate effectively is an important part of almost every professional position and is a highly valued skill that employers look for in applicants. The following words and phrases are ones that you can use when describing your communication skills and related traits:

- confident
- friendly
- respectful
- clear
- concise
- empathetic
- open-minded
- active listener
- interpersonal skills
- writing skills
- verbal and nonverbal communication

Flexibility

A lot of positions need at least some flexibility, as procedures and situations are certainly going to change at some point in your career path. Having the ability to quickly and effectively adapt to new situations is a valuable trait to employers and ensures that you can work with various people in differing situations and environments. Below are a few strong words related to flexibility that are useful to your next job interview:

- flexible
- adaptable

- quick learner
- solution-oriented
- positive
- conflict-resolver
- problem-solver
- open communicator
- accountable
- resilient

Leadership

Another skill that is sought after by employers is leadership, especially if you are interviewing for a leadership position, so it is important that you use strong words to showcase this skill. Good words for leadership include the following:

- coordinate
- accomplish
- initiate
- deliver
- accelerate
- negotiate
- resolve
- develop
- plan
- innovate
- supervise
- build

Passion

The people who are hiring will want to know that you are passionate about the position that you've applied for and that same passion will support your success in the role. Passionate people are more likely to excel in their careers and support company growth.

Words that emphasize your own passion for a job include:

- passionate
- interested
- enthusiastic
- motivated
- driven
- energized
- love
- priority
- win

Responsibility

This is another important trait that interviewers look for in potential employees; no matter what position you're applying for, they will want to know if you are willing to finish your tasks and take responsibility for your work and your actions. The following words and phrases can help you successfully tell the interviewers how responsible you are:

- provide
- responsible
- results-oriented
- efficient
- effective
- maintain
- accomplish
- detail-oriented
- organized
- reorganize
- prepare
- works well on tight deadlines
- met the deadline
- team player

- committed to excellence on time
- practical
- satisfied the client's requests
- solution
- support

Teamwork

At least some level of teamwork is required by many positions; this is especially true if you are applying for a leadership role, or at least a role that's directly part of a team. Showing your teamwork abilities through powerful words can help demonstrate your teamwork abilities and commitment to working effectively with others. Great words to use for teamwork include:

- communication
- cooperation
- tolerance
- collaboration
- emotional intelligence
- influence
- initiative
- persuade
- flexibility
- trustworthy

Industry Buzzwords and Jargon

Every industry comes with their own buzzwords, but if you're outside a certain field then the jargon can make you feel a little confused, like some kind of code that's keeping you from understanding the conversation. However, if you are in the know and the jargon is familiar, using it during a conversation is similar to a secret handshake, as it lets interviewers know that you do in fact understand the industry.

For example, if you were interviewing for a marketing position, you might include keywords such as conversion rate, key performance metrics, pay per click (PPC), return on investment (ROI), and paid media. It demonstrates competency in your field and that you understand the duties that you will be responsible for in a marketing position.

To use jargon, you naturally have to actually understand it; so, if you are new to a field or industry, then you should familiarize yourself with its lingo. You should also follow people from the same industry on Twitter, connect with them on LinkedIn, and look for relevant blogs and videos.

Words Reflecting Company Values

If you really want to show a company that you're a good fit then you should mirror the words that the company uses to describe itself; there is a high likelihood that these same phrases are used with frequency in internal communications and company meetings.

Even if interviewers don't realize on a conscious level that you are reflecting their own words back at them, it will still make a subtle yet positive impression. Your best bet is to examine the language used on the company's "About Me" webpage, on social media pages, and within the job's advertisement.

But, interviewers aren't going to be impressed if you sound like you simply memorized the company's version; in order to help them understand that you are what they are looking for, you are free to use synonyms.

You now have knowledge of the most commonly used powerful words; but naturally, this isn't the whole list. In the additional materials of this book, you'll find lists of action verbs, adjectives, and soft skills, which will be a great weapon when they are used in cover letters and resumes, or during job interviews. While you practice your responses to the questions, keep your ears open to your verb choices. Do certain, less powerful words like "help" keep coming up? Use more powerful verbs. You should also choose strong descriptive words and phrases as well; a project can be "a success" or it can be "award winning;" it can "perform well" or "result in a 40% jump in sales."

The best words to use in your answers to the interviewer will be dependent on what role you are applying for; if you're applying as an accountant, for instance, you will want to integrate a bunch of words that show that you're great with numbers and don't make a lot of mistakes, but also focus less on words that demonstrate leadership ability, unless it's for a job as an accounting manager.

Bear in mind that it's not only during interviews that word choice matters; do opt for those powerful action words in your cover letter and resume too.

CHAPTER 8

How to Answer Behavioral Questions During Interviews

4-Step Technique

Behavioral questions are typically open-ended; they can cover a pretty wide range, and it is not possible to prepare yourself for every question that can be asked. What does help is to be able to relate the question to the commonly asked interview questions that you have already prepared for and answer accordingly. The four-step process below will help you with answering a behavioral question during an interview.

We will be using the following example question:

"Have you ever had trouble getting people to accept your ideas? How did you approach this problem and did you come to a successful solution?"

Step 1: Understand the Question

The first thing you do when you are given a behavioral question is to listen carefully and understand it. It is good practice to reiterate the question in your own words and ask the interviewer if this is what they meant. If there is any confusion, clarify it by asking follow-up questions. Once you understand the question, ask yourself the same question in simpler words.

Step 2: Extract the Keywords

The next step is to extract useful keywords from the question that will help you with shortlisting your stories. In regards to the example question, we can say that the keywords are *Leadership*, *Conflict Resolution*, and *Communication*.

Step 3: Select the Story

From the shortlisted stories, choose the one that best describes the question and hadn't so far been used in the interview.

Step 4: Apply the STAR Method

Apply the STAR method to the shortlisted story, as described in Step 5 of *Chapter 6*.

4-Step Technique

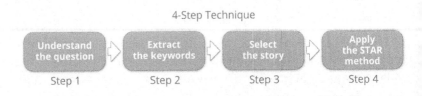

| Understand the question | Extract the keywords | Select the story | Apply the STAR method |
| Step 1 | Step 2 | Step 3 | Step 4 |

Answering Trick Questions

At times, you might be asked a particularly tricky question that you aren't prepared to answer. What do you do in this case? There is a solution for occasions like this.

Here are three things to keep in mind that should help you with this:

1. Firstly, don't panic!

2. Remember that it is alright to say, *"That's a difficult question, let me think for a minute."* No interviewer should fault you for requesting this once or twice during an interview. If you receive a difficult question, don't rush yourself and simply blurt out an answer just for the sake of not looking silly; take a deep breath and think it through.

3. Finally, for a lot of these questions, the interviewer will just want to hear about your thought process; explain how you would approach the situation and the reasoning behind your response.

Below are a few examples of difficult questions and some advice on how to answer them.

1. *"Tell me about the worst manager that you've ever had; how did you navigate around them?"*

One thing that you should never do in an interview is talk badly about previous employers. Besides being in poor taste to do so, another reason to avoid this behavior is that your interviewer has your resume and knows where you have worked, so your previous bosses are not completely anonymous. To help get around this, you might explain to the interviewer that your previous bosses' management styles simply weren't ideal for you. If you've never had a bad manager, don't make one up just to answer the question. Let the interviewer know that you have honestly gotten along with your previous managers, and focus on how you have been able to work successfully with different personalities and management styles.

2. "If a coworker had an annoying habit and it was in the way of you giving excellent work quality, how would you resolve it?"

A question like this is asked so the interviewer can get a feel for how you deal with others. Expanding on the previous point, you shouldn't talk badly about either current or former coworkers. To answer this question, draw from a real-life experience if possible. What annoyed you? How was it resolved? If it happened again, is there a more effective way to handle the situation? Identify the annoying habit and then outline the steps that you would take to try to resolve the situation while keeping a good relationship with your coworker.

3. "Tell me about a time when you didn't agree with a company policy."

While you should again avoid giving an overly negative response to this question, to say that you've never disagreed with a company policy could be difficult to believe from the interviewer's point of view, no matter how amenable the employee appears. In addition, it sends a message that you are someone who might simply accept anything that you are told to do without thinking about all the possible outcomes. While companies want leaders and employees to follow the rules, they also want people who will review any possibly outdated policies and have the courage to stand up and propose changes to maintain a current, competitive edge and productive workplace. So, what response are they looking for? Talk about a time that you opposed a policy for a reason that is business-related and logical; touch on the research that you conducted, the facts that you presented, and the outcome of your attempts to have the policy rewritten.

CHAPTER 9

20 Most Common Behavioral Interview Questions and Strategies for Answering Them

Leadership Questions

Leadership-related questions are among the common types of questions related to behavior. These qualities are treasured by employers and some will even build their whole interview process around them. However, wonderful leaders are those who do more than just tell people what to do; they bring value by creating an environment that is collaborative and supportive. A great leader is someone who sees and helps build the skills of those around them; they boost morale and promote productivity.

When interviewers ask about leadership, they are looking for certain qualities, which include:

- **Ability to innovate:** *Leaders come up with new ideas.*
- **Ability to influence and inspire:** *Leaders can optimize their coworkers' potential; they will commend extraordinary efforts*

and lead the way through their hard work and dedication.

- **Conflict resolution:** *Leaders support their coworkers through difficult times and help find solutions to relational problems.*

- **Organization and decision-making skills**: *Leaders have the ability to manage people and projects in a productive manner, and contribute to the company's commercial goals.*

- **Effectiveness:** *Leaders can push to overcome obstacles and effect the implementation of changes.*

- **Self-awareness:** *Leaders are confident in their abilities, yet are able to recognize their limits. Good leaders will delegate and trust the advice given to them by their coworkers.*

- **Self-confidence:** *Leaders are never afraid to take responsibility.*

Many job seekers will make the mistake of believing that if they aren't looking for a management role, they will dodge being asked leadership questions. In reality, employers are looking for potential leaders at any employment level, including entry and graduate levels.

Businesses will look for employees who are likely to progress within the company, so your interviewer will ask you management-related questions to determine whether you are a good long-term investment for them. So, whatever your experience level is, it is important that you prepare for behavioral leadership questions by speaking about specific times when you have demonstrated leadership qualities.

SAMPLE QUESTION #1

"Tell me about a time you demonstrated leadership/initiative on the job."

Situation: *"In my previous role, one of my responsibilities was to gather sales data. During the end of the previous financial year, I saw that sales for a particular product were falling behind our expectations."*

Task: *"I needed to find a way to address this issue."*

Action: *"I took charge by calling a team meeting. I made the suggestion that we design a package that contained a few deals that we could use to offer our clients bulk quantities of the falling product for discounted prices. I also decided to schedule weekly meetings with my coworkers to check up on our sales and listen to any concerns that may have arisen."*

Result: *"Our customers were quite responsive to our packages; not only had our sales recovered by the new year's second quarter, the profits for the product had risen by 15%. The team was rewarded handsomely for the boost in our sales numbers and it made us even more eager to improve our performance further."*

SAMPLE QUESTION #2

"Describe a time when you had to motivate coworkers."

Situation: *"We went through a company merger last year that lowered the morale of some of our teams. Our team had new management that handed us responsibilities that we had little experience with."*

Task: *"I felt that I had to do something about our new situation after I noticed a dip in our overall productivity."*

Action: *"I called a team meeting and inspired the team to welcome the learning opportunities and see this as career development. All of us in the room took a turn to list one positive thing that we gained from the experience."*

Result: *"Everyone's mood was uplifted after that, and the positivity transformed into better productivity and engagement."*

Possible questions on leadership

- *Tell me about a time you led a project.*
- *Tell me about a time when you successfully delegated tasks to your team.*
- *Describe a time when you showed initiative and caused others to follow.*

- *Describe a time when you had to take over the leadership role in the middle of a project.*
- *Tell me about someone you have personally mentored.*
- *Describe a time when you had to make an unpopular decision.*

Teamwork Questions

Teamwork is another prerequisite for many employers, so be prepared to talk about your ability to work with others to ensure that you can answer appropriately to teamwork-related questions.

Interviewers use this category of questions when positive teamwork is an important part of their work environment and company culture. In a lot of industries, the performance of team members in effective collaborations is important to operational success and productivity. If you are a person who would rather work independently and are lacking in interpersonal "people" skills, then you might not be the best candidate for the job.

Below are some teamwork skills that you'll want to bear in mind as you prepare for answering teamwork-related questions:

- conflict management
- communication
- active listening
- delegating
- reliability
- mediating conflicts
- monitoring progress
- respectfulness

Before your interview takes place, come up with at least a couple of team situations where you showed some of the listed teamwork skills. At the least, one of the examples should consist of a moment when you helped solve a challenge or problem that the group was having difficulty with. You shouldn't limit yourself to examples from paid employment situations if you are someone with a sparse work history; consider other settings such as group projects for volunteer organizations, clubs, and classes.

In your answer, you will want to focus on how you were helpful within the group achieving the result; try not to focus too much on your individual success, as you are trying to demonstrate that you are a team player. Don't use the kinds of answers that imply that the team only succeeded because of your contribution.

SAMPLE QUESTION #3

"Give me an example of when you worked well with a team."

Situation: *"My previous employers noticed that monthly sales had been stagnating throughout the entire financial quarter. They discussed in a meeting amongst themselves their concerns as to what it could mean for the next quarter."*

Task: *"At the time, I was working on a sales team and we were required to increase our monthly sales profits at the request of our employers."*

Action: *"I began a weekly meeting where we would brainstorm and share ideas for new sales tactics. There were no bad ideas; however, some of the ideas had to be discarded as they would have been difficult to implement."*

Result: *"At the end, several of the team's ideas were implemented, and we ended up defeating our sales target by 20%. Our employers were so pleased by our handling of the situation that we received a 5% bonus and glowing performance reviews."*

SAMPLE QUESTION #4

"Tell me about a time when you collaborated with others who were different than you."

Situation: *"I enjoy working with different people, because they usually bring something new to the table. At a previous job there was a new and young developer who was assigned to work with me on a new project for software development, and I was tasked with* *walking him through our standard coding process."*

Task: *"In order to work together effectively, I had to get to know him and find common ground. Despite him being younger than me, it wasn't an issue, because he was completely self-taught; he didn't know a lot about our industry methodologies."*

Action: *"It would have taken too much time to teach him everything from scratch; instead, I briefly explained the development process that we were using for that specific project and taught him how to write the tests for our code-base. Doing these tests is the best way to learn, and it is the way that I started with development."*

Result: *"I also sat down and helped him go through the material sometimes, but in the end, he surprised me by how fast a learner he was; he only needed a little encouragement and guidance. He learned the entire process in under a week, and I learned a bit about multitasking and time management from him."*

Possible questions on teamwork

- *Tell me about a time you disagreed with another team member.*
- *Tell me about a time when you showed strong teamwork skills.*
- *Tell me about how you react if you feel that a team member isn't doing their job.*
- *Tell me about a time when your team was storming and performing as one.*
- *Have you ever worked with a manager who was pulling in a different direction?*
- *Can you give me an example of how you've contributed to the culture of previous teams, companies or groups?*

Problem-Solving Questions

Interviewers will ask behavioral questions in relation to problem-solving in order to get a better understanding of how you work.

Are you the type who is driven to look for ways to contribute? Can you help your team perform better? Can you help to improve things or do you just sit around waiting for instructions?

What the interviewer is looking for is a general problem-solving orientation to your personality; for many jobs, the interviewer is also looking for a provable record of overcoming different types of challenges that are commonly found in the role.

For example, a representative in customer service should be able to handle an angry customer; a project manager should be able to handle a change in deadline; and a senior-level operations individual should be able to fix a process that is considered inefficient.

If you haven't prepared in advance, you can be thrown off by this kind of behavioral question because it can be a little difficult to pull up a strong example, along with the relevant details on the spot. Below are a few tips for how you can handle these types of questions:

- Think about the most impressive challenges you've overcome, your most creative approaches, and the solutions that made the biggest difference for the company.
- Stick with stories that match the job description; they can come in the form of job-specific problems or higher-level strategic issues.
- Don't raise red flags by talking about problems that you either caused or contributed to in a negative way.
- To stand out from the crowd, you should provide enough detail to provide a sense of who you are and how you think.

SAMPLE QUESTION #5

"Tell me about a time when you handled a challenging situation."

Situation: *"I was a retail manager at a department store. During one prom season, there was an instance when a customer bought a dress online and had requested to have it delivered to the store.*

However, one of my associates mistakenly put it out on the floor, where it was purchased right away by another customer."

Task: *"I knew that I had to make this right for the customer in order to meet my personal level of service standards as well as holding up the company's reputation."*

Action: *"Before I made the call to the customer to apologize for the mistake, I managed to locate the same dress at another store nearby. I requested that it be delivered to her home the morning of prom night, along with a gift card as a thank you for her understanding."*

Result: *"The customer was so grateful that she wrote us a five-star review on several review sites. We also had an influx of new customers next prom season because of those reviews."*

SAMPLE QUESTION #6

"Describe a time when you had to solve a problem but didn't have all the necessary information about it beforehand. What did you do?"

Situation: *"When I was working as an office manager, the company CEO came to me and I was informed that employee productivity was down. They were concerned as to how it would affect the future of the company."*

Task: *"He asked me to find a solution."*

Action: *"I decided to ask the team members about their work lives by conducting interviews and sending out short surveys. After I analyzed all of the information, I discovered that the employees had no way to keep track of and organize tasks. I gave the recommendation to the CEO of implementing a new project management system."*

Result: *"After the new system was implemented, our productivity increased by 10%. In addition, the employees felt a further sense of satisfaction from having their work unburdened."*

Possible questions on problem solving

- *Describe a time when you had to do something for which you were not trained or had no experience.*

- *Give an example of a time you made a decision that was unpopular and explain how you handled implementing it.*

- *Give an example of when you had to be very strategic in your tasks to meet all of your responsibilities under a specific deadline.*

- *Share an example of a time you had to manage multiple competing priorities*

- *Please describe a time when you faced a significant obstacle to succeeding with an important work project or activity.*

- *Tell me about a time when you used creativity to overcome a dilemma.*

Accomplishment Questions

"What is your greatest accomplishment?" and similar questions are asked in order to receive insight about a candidate's proven work and what achievements they view as most valuable and important. When you are asked by an interviewer about your greatest accomplishment, their interest lies in learning about three primary things:

- **Your work ethic:** Interviewers want to know what you consider an "accomplishment" and the proven work that you completed to achieve it.

- **Your core values:** Interviewers are interested in which accomplishment you choose as your "greatest," and why.

- **Your work examples:** Interviewers wish to learn about your specific work-related examples, to give them an idea of the projects that you have completed and what they can anticipate from you.

If you are asked about your accomplishments, see it as the perfect opportunity to talk about your most impressive achievements.

Unfortunately, most candidates tend to waste the opportunity because they aren't prepared to answer and/or don't feel comfortable with "bragging." In general, most people don't have enough practice speaking about their greatest accomplishments.

For people who are modest and/or introverted, this can be quite a challenge. You might even have previously learned that it is obnoxious and/or rude to gloat about your accomplishments. However, if you can't let go of the discomfort of talking about your achievements, you are not giving yourself the opportunity that you deserve.

Good stories about your accomplishments can be used to answer behavioral questions in multiple categories. For example, a story about a successful project can demonstrate conflict resolution, leadership, or problem-solving. Here are a few questions to ask yourself when identifying accomplishments that you can talk about:

- How did you contribute to company goals in previous jobs? Perhaps you had a huge impact on a key performance indicator, such as increased revenue.

- What impact did you have on a team as a manager, mentor, or team player? Maybe you helped an intern and set them up for success, which in turn benefited the company as a whole.

- How did you help your company become more efficient? You might have led improvements to the process by enhancing communication channels.

- What did you do to enhance the customer experience? You could have helped innovate a new solution that was user-centric.

- If you are new to the workforce: Did you ever take the lead on anything at a student organization or while doing volunteer work? Perhaps you organized an event, won a competition, or even raised money for a good cause.

- If your interviewer specifically asks for a non-work example: Beyond the office, what personal goals have you met? You might have finished a long distance marathon, or you overcame a personal challenge of some kind.

If it is hard for you to choose one achievement that feels like the "greatest" one, go back to your research and think about it from the point of view of the interviewer that you are trying to impress and the job that you are trying to get. Below are a few mistakes to avoid:

- Don't emphasize your part in group achievements or take credit for a team effort on projects.
- Don't simply brag about what you've done or let your ego control you.
- Don't "wing it," as not preparing a good answer ahead of time can stall your interview.
- Don't say that you don't have any accomplishments, even if you recently graduated from school.
- Don't include confidential information about previous employers when answering.

SAMPLE QUESTION #7

"What is your greatest accomplishment?"

Situation: *"My greatest accomplishment was when I helped convince a small town in Oregon to switch from their antique street lighting to the energy-efficient LED bulbs that my company produced."*

Task: *"My role was to promote and sell the bulbs, while speaking about the long-term advantage of the reduced energy costs. However, my role had been recently developed, so I had to come up with a strategy to educate the officials on the value of the bulbs; this was a challenge, as our products had an expensive up-front cost in comparison to inefficient lighting options."*

Action: *"I created and distributed an information packet and assembled events for the local community that were geared toward the city officials and the public. I demoed the company product during these events and answered questions, which emphasized the value of the bulbs for long-term use. I was able to influence a wide range of community members with these events and, in a small town, it is always important to have the public on board."*

Result: *"I was able to reach my sales goal of $100,000 for my first year, and I gained my company another contract from a nearby city that was interested in our energy-efficient bulbs. In addition, this communication strategy that focused on the community gained us attention from the national media. I am also proud to say I got a promotion within a year to the position of Senior Sales Representative."*

SAMPLE QUESTION #8

"What achievement are you most proud of?"

Situation: *"While I was working as a mechanic at my previous employment, vehicles would regularly come in with problems that were hard to diagnose. We had one truck that was brought to the shop several times with an electrical issue that no other mechanic could pinpoint the cause of."*

Task: *"At the request of my floor manager, I took a look at the vehicle to see if I could determine the root cause."*

Action: *"I spent some time examining the truck and doing extensive research online and through the manufacturer for any possible solutions to this electrical issue. It was admittedly a time-consuming task, as it took nearly three days before my research bore fruit."*

Result: *"After I had explored every piece of documentation that I could find about this make and model of truck, I determined the cause of the problem. I was able to figure out a workable solution that ensured that it would not happen again for the client, providing exceptional customer service."*

Possible phrasing of questions on accomplishment

- Tell me about your proudest professional accomplishment.
- What's your proudest moment at work?
- What were the biggest wins in your most recent role?
- What work are you most proud of?
- What would you consider your most impressive achievement?
- Can you describe an important goal you accomplished?

Work Ethic Questions

In order to have a good work performance, one needs to have a good work ethic. Having a good work ethic means that one must follow a set of moral values, behaviors, and principles, which in turn determines whether or not you make the "morally right" decision when you are faced with a job-related situation.

Being able to recognize a strong work ethic is a key to differentiating between the top performers and the average job candidates. Even if a candidate has significant experience and required skills, there is still no guarantee that they will be hired unless they are able to demonstrate a strong work ethic.

In order to have a strong work ethic, employees must show that they are determined to meet the company's goals; however, they must do so while they are following the rules and regulations that have been set by the company. Employees with a strong work ethic are dedicated, hardworking, and reliable in delivering their best work on time; in essence, employees who possess a strong work ethic are the ones who are motivated to work hard and smart.

The following list describes the top characteristics typically associated with a strong work ethic:

1. **Hard work.** Employees with a strong work ethic are hardworking; they will often go the distance, if not further, to excel at their tasks.

2. **High productivity.** Employees with a strong work ethic tend to use their time in ways that are both efficient and effective in completing their tasks.

3. **Reliability.** Employees with a strong work ethic are reliable; employers know that they can rely on them to complete their tasks when they are asked to do so.

4. **Dedication.** Employees with a strong work ethic are dedicated to their job and will often go above and beyond what is initially required of them.

5. Responsibility. Employees with a strong work ethic will adhere to the policies and rules of the workplace as well as taking responsibility for their behavior.

6. Punctuality. Employees with a strong work ethic will always give consideration to deadlines and finish all of their tasks on time.

In the majority of positions, "work ethic" isn't the number-one quality written in the description; interviewers will first trim down their list of applicants based on their experience and skills.

If an interview is in your future, you should know that it is because you possess the basic qualifications; however, what matters is demonstrating how you "stand out from the crowd" in comparison to the other applicants, who are also qualified.

Quite a bit of the last cut has to do with "fitting in," and one's work ethic plays a huge role in whether or not you'll be able to fit into the job, as well as with the team and the company culture.

To demonstrate your fit for a job that requires a strong work ethic, it is important to be able to talk about a provable record of putting in that extra effort to achieve impressive results. Here are some examples that can highlight work ethic:

- To meet a tight deadline, you put in an extraordinary amount of effort to achieve the time crunch (stayed late, took on additional tasks, learned a new skill, fixed someone else's mistakes, etc.)
- You helped the team succeed in their goals by adding on additional responsibilities for yourself.
- You put in extra time and effort to improve something instead of settling for what would be considered "good enough."
- You pushed through when the odds were stacked against you and it would have been easy to give up.

SAMPLE QUESTION #9

"Tell me about a time when you went above and beyond your duties for a job or task."

Situation: *"During my time as a real estate agent, we received one of the biggest listings the company had ever had. It was a house that was newly built, worth $5M, and was ready to go on the market."*

Task: *"We only had a three-month deadline from the owner to sell it, so all agents were given the go-ahead to work on selling the property."*

Action: *"I made the decision to add something new to the website marketing of the house: a virtual tour. I felt that the photos weren't enough to sell the property. I rented a 360° camera and taught myself to create the tour by staying up and watching tutorials."*

Result: *"When I presented it to management, they were thrilled; they put the tour up on the website and also asked the agents to send it out to their lists of clients. The person who ultimately bought the house had been in Europe at the time and hadn't even come to see the house before they purchased it. He said that this client felt like he'd already been in the house because of the tour and had no doubts about purchasing it."*

SAMPLE QUESTION #10

"Tell me about a time when you made a suggestion to improve the quality/quantity of the work in your last workplace."

Situation: *"At my previous company, the leadership team was always making changes in an effort to improve the quality of service that we provided. However, it never seemed like these changes stuck around for very long."*

Task: *"There was never any follow-up and the employees would just revert back to doing things the way they always had."*

Action: *"I made a suggestion that we implement a binder filled with these changes in order to keep track of them. That way, it would be easier to check on which ones worked and which ones didn't, as well as helping to ensure that the changes were implemented each week."*

Result: *"Because of the binder, the results were now clearer and the more successful adjustments became the standard policy that all employees followed. My employers were so impressed that I received a 20% bonus."*

Possible questions on work ethic

- *Tell me about the most uncomfortable or difficult thing you've had to do at work.*
- *Give an example of when you completed a difficult task that made you work harder than normal.*
- *Tell me a time when you identified a problem with a process and what steps did you take to improve the problem?*
- *Describe a time that you felt overwhelmed with your workload and how you handled it.*
- *Can you describe a time when you went the extra mile at work?*
- *Tell me about a time when you identified a new, unusual or different approach for addressing a problem or task.*
- *When things are slow at work or you've finished your tasks, what do you do?*

Conflict Resolution Questions

Another common category of behavioral questions is related to how a candidate provides resolution to a conflict. The idea behind this is for the interviewer to discover your ability to handle conflict with coworkers and supervisors, how you handle conflict in general, and your interpersonal skills in the workplace.

What type of conflict handler are you?

- Are you someone who tries to avoid conflicts whenever they come up?
- Are you someone who pretends that there is no conflict and ignores the situation?
- Are you someone who goes with the flow and is the accommodating type?

- Are you someone who sees conflict as an opportunity to compromise and collaborate?

The interviewer will be interested in your approach to handling conflict situations and how you handled them in the past. They want to find out how you react in certain work situations, such as:

- with a coworker
- with the boss/supervisor
- with the team
- between two colleagues
- with client/customer

Any one of these can be a theme of conflict resolution questions.

You can integrate several of these skills into your answers. A few you might be able to think of on the spot and others you may already have used before, but it is important that you provide the interviewer with a clear response on how you approach conflict resolution. These are the most important conflict resolution skills:

- **Asking questions and active listening.** Asking the right questions and listening carefully to what the people involved are saying is a crucial part in resolving conflicts. It is through this process that you are most likely to gain an understanding of the origin of the complaint and how you should go about solving it.

- **Problem-solving.** Problem-solving skills help with determining the source of a conflict or problem and finding an effective way to solve it. For example, problem-solving skills can be used to identify certain areas of compromise between the people involved in the disagreement.

- **Perspective and empathy.** These pertain to being able to understand another person's feelings and viewpoints; this is an important part of resolving conflicts. If you can understand other people's observations, thoughts, and triggers, you are more likely to be able to resolve the conflict.

- **Facilitating a productive dialogue.** The first step in resolving a conflict is being able to get people to open up in order to facilitate a productive dialogue. Communication is always an important part of bringing cohesion to moments of conflict.

- **Assertiveness.** Assertive behavior is a form of communication; it helps others in a way that is direct, honest, and open. Being assertive refers to being able to stand up for either your own or the rights of others in a positive and calm way; it is a valuable skill to have and emphasize in your answers.

- **Mediation.** Bringing positivity to the work environment is done by employees who are considerate of other people's feelings and thoughts, and are kind and open-minded. Empathy is important in various jobs, but especially in positions related to customer service.

When you are answering these kinds of questions, there are three mistakes that you need to avoid:

- Don't say that you get along with everyone and have never been faced with a work conflict.

- Don't use answers that make you appear unreasonable or difficult to work with.

- Don't use your response to shift blame onto others or to cast past bosses or coworkers in a negative light.

SAMPLE QUESTION #11

"Tell me about a time you had a conflict at work."

Situation: *"In my previous role, I had a colleague that was consistently late and my team had to wait for them in order to begin our daily tasks. I could tell that my teammates' patience was dwindling, and I was concerned as to what that would do to the team morale and our workload."*

Task: *"I decided to take the initiative and approached my colleague to discuss why she could not make it to our morning meetings on time."*

Action: *"After some disagreement about her lateness, I offered an alternative solution that would suit her and keep the team on schedule. She calmed down and explained that she had a legitimate* excuse for being late and that she would welcome any solution that I suggested."

Result: *"In the end, I arranged to have our morning team meeting time adjusted to mid-morning to allow for any lateness or pressing tasks that may interfere in the future. In this way, all of the team members could attend and participate fully every day."*

SAMPLE QUESTION #12

"Have you ever had to mediate a conflict between two colleagues?"

Situation: *"A few months back, two of our sales reps were continually bickering with each other. The bickering had started out as teasing but quickly escalated, and it made them very unpleasant to work with."*

Task: *"While I was also a sales rep, and neither of them reported to me, I decided to approach them individually and get to the root of their disagreements."*

Action: *"I listened intently to each of their points of view. Then I suggested that the three of us sit down together, where I acted as a mediator and got them both to talk about what was bothering them."*

Result: *"In the end, we were able to uncover the root cause of their disconnection and I helped to coach them in a meaningful conversation. This experience also taught me about how to resolve conflicts, which in turn boosted my confidence to apply for the assistant manager promotion shortly after. And since then, I have taken a weekend workshop on interpersonal conflict management."*

Possible questions on conflict resolution

- *Have you ever disagreed and resolved a conflict with your boss?*
- *Share an example of a team conflict. How did you resolve it?*
- *Tell me about a time when you have worked with others who thought differently.*

- *Tell me about a time when you had to deal with an angry or dissatisfied customer.*
- *Tell me about a time that you disagreed with a rule or approach.*
- *How do you deal with different opinions when working on a team?*

Failure Questions

Questions regarding past mistakes are some of the toughest and trickiest interview questions to answer. You do want to acknowledge the mistake, but without bad-mouthing or blaming other people; you also never want to make yourself look like a liability or too risky to hire.

You need to avoid talking about mistakes involving carelessness or lack of effort. It is better to talk about making a mistake because you had never experienced the situation before, or didn't have the right knowledge. Another key is to talk about what you learned from the experience as well as how you've improved since then.

If it is possible, speak about encountering a situation that is similar a second time and getting an even better outcome because of the lessons that you've learned. In addition, you'll receive bonus points if you sound humble, so speak modestly. You should also convey appreciation for the lesson that you've learned, even though experiencing a failure is never fun at the time it occurs.

If you do these things, you'll have an excellent answer that will impress the interviewer. There are several main elements that interviewers will look for in your answer, such as:

- exactly what the failure was
- if the failure was avoidable or not
- your actions in remedying the situation
- how you plan to avoid those kinds of issues in the future, especially as their employee

As vital as it is to be honest in your answer, it is equally so to follow up with a well-thought-out solution to such issues in the future.

Good answers to questions about failure will include several things:

- your mistake
- the lesson you learned after the fact
- how you change going forward
- eloquence and honesty
- a solution that is related to the position you are interviewing for
- a compelling story that engages your listener

Your answer needs to be both brief and detailed enough to give your interviewer a vision of the bigger picture. Was a lesson learned? How did you learn it? Has the experience made you a better employee in that particular field, industry, or position?

One might certainly answer the question "incorrectly" or in a not very good way; luckily, the majority of the wrong answers you need to steer away from have more to do with common sense. Bad answers to avoid include:

- *"I have never failed professionally before."*
- *"I caused the downfall of an entire company."*
- *"I did some dirty work or engaged in illegal activities that got me fired."*
- *"I failed at X, Y, and Z, but it wasn't my fault."*
- *"I failed at X, Y, and Z in my last position and simply decided to change positions or industries to avoid such a mistake again."*

If you are able to avoid these answers and similar ones, then you'll be just fine.

SAMPLE QUESTION #13

"Tell me about a time you failed/made a mistake."

Situation: *"A short time after I was promoted to senior project manager, I was in charge of leading a project for a major client. A* project like this would typically take about a month to complete, but the client was in a rush and asked if I could have it ready in three weeks."

Task: "Letting my excitement about my first project overwhelm me, I hastily agreed and set the ambitious deadline of three weeks to prove myself to them. However, I realized shortly after that I'd need a bit more time to finish it and be able to deliver quality work."

Action: "I reached out to the client immediately and apologized. In addition, I also asked for a three-day extension, and they were generous enough to extend the deadline."

Result: "I was able to finish the project and deliver it before the extended deadline. From this, I learned how to manage my time better and never over-promise on something I wouldn't be able to deliver."

SAMPLE QUESTION #14

"What is your biggest regret at work?"

Situation: "In my last job, I was responsible for supervising the company's IT team. There was one particular team member who was always late to both work and deadlines. At the time, it had never caused any major problems and they did contribute some of the best work on the team."

Task: "So I avoided saying anything to them, and I believe that my inaction contributed to his eventual failure on important deadlines and projects; it eventually cost us a big client and my manager ended up firing him."

Action: "I regret that I had not talked to him personally; I believe that if I had, this entire incident could have been avoided and he still would have been employed there. Also, we would have kept that client with our company."

Result: "The entire situation made me realize that, as a supervisor, I am responsible for my team. If I ever find myself in a situation like *this again, I will immediately talk to the team member in a way that is approachable, but firm."*

Possible phrasing of questions on failure

- *Describe an occasion when you failed at something. What did you learn?*
- *Can you detail a mistake you made and how you reacted to it?*
- *Have you ever made a mistake?*
- *Tell me of a time when you didn't meet your goals.*
- *Are you someone who learns from failures?*
- *Tell me about a time when you tried something risky and failed.*
- *Tell me about a decision that you've regretted and how you overcame it.*
- *How did you handle a previous mistake?*

Other Common Questions

SAMPLE QUESTION #15

"Describe a time when you were under a lot of pressure at work."

This is a behavioral interview question about stress management. The ability to work under pressure is an extremely valuable quality. Being able to give an appropriate response may help your chances of being hired. A question like this gives you the chance to show how well you perform under pressure when the circumstances are difficult.

Being able to convince your interviewer that you can do a good job under pressure can also suggest to them that you have other good qualities, such as organizational and time management skills, quick decision-making, and even problem-solving abilities. But even if you are confident of your ability to work under pressure, the point of your answer is to convince your potential employer of that. Below are some ideas for you to consider when preparing to answer this question:

- **Think of how you handle stress.** While you are working under pressure, you need ways to help lower your stress levels. When you are crafting your response, think of what strategies you use to stay calm in high-pressure situations. You could share the relaxation techniques you use, like meditation; you could also discuss how your time management skills help you to avoid stress.

- **Show that stress motivates you.** Interviewers ask you this question to learn how you work in stressful conditions. You can put a positive spin on your answer by sharing how a bit of stress is actually motivating for you; mention how, when the stakes are high, you become more driven and motivated to do a good job.

- **Stay calm and cool.** Interviewers will often observe your nonverbal cues; since the interview itself can be considered a high-pressure situation, answering these questions in a manner that is calm and confident is crucial. As you're verbally expressing your confidence, your demeanor and tone should match up with your words. This might aid you in gaining the interviewer's trust and help them to feel confident that you are also being truthful with the rest of your answers.

Now, before you get interviewed, it is also of importance to know what not to say. Below are some common mistakes that applicants make when they're answering this question:

- **"I never get stressed."** Yes, everyone does get stressed and giving this answer will make the interviewer believe that you are being duplicitous. If you love working under pressure, that's fine; do state that pressure impacts you in a positive way and then support your response with specifics.

- **Not tailoring your answer to the specific job.** What needs to be kept in mind is the end game, which is landing the specific job that you are interviewing for. If you are being interviewed for a managerial position, never say that managing people and/or projects is stressful for you, and never say *"I delegate."*

Being able to manage your own stress doesn't refer to adding onto others'.

- **Answering with too much honesty.** Not all people are capable of thriving under pressure and that's fine, but it is a problem when you are being too honest. For people who are the type to crumble under pressure, don't tell the interviewer that; instead, keep their focus on how you deal with stress and how you will continue to improve, rather than how badly it makes you feel.

- **Share an example when you had created the pressure.** When talking about your past in regards to working under pressure, the pressure itself should have been due to outside forces. You don't want a potential employer thinking that you create your own stress, or worse yet, that you are a source of stress for your colleagues.

SAMPLE ANSWER to the question *"Describe a time when you were under a lot of pressure at work."*

Situation: *"I am in the habit of adopting the ability to work under pressure because it forces me to alter into the best version of myself and to act in a quick and decisive manner. At my previous job, I was informed that a major client was arriving from overseas and that I had only five hours to prepare for them."*

Task: *"I was tasked with creating a presentation for their arrival."*

Action: *"I quickly shook myself out of my initial feelings of panic, took a deep breath and settled my thoughts, and decided on the best way of working on such short notice. It was an intense and stressful five hours."*

Result: *"But in the end, I managed to create a powerful presentation. I know that stress has a tendency to build up; however, I eliminate it through practicing meditation and yoga. Reading also relaxes me after a long day of work, renewing my mind and making me ready to take on whatever comes my way the next day."*

Possible questions on stress management

- *Do you work well under pressure?*
- *What's the most stressful situation you've faced at work?*
- *How do you handle unexpected changes or challenges?*
- *Tell me about a time when you were overwhelmed at work. How did you handle it?*
- *Tell me a time when you had to work unexpectedly on your own.*
- *Describe a scenario where you've had to make a quick decision in the workplace.*

SAMPLE QUESTION #16

"Describe a situation when you had to learn something new on the spot."

This is a behavioral interview question that is asking about adaptability; in today's competitive markets, it is important for companies to have employees in their workforce that are able to adapt to changing work environments. People who are adaptable have an easier time accepting changes to working procedures and team environments. Also, when the unexpected occurs, they are able to come up with effective solutions to aid them toward their goals. In addition, those who are adaptable are more likely to stay calm under pressure and work their way through dynamic environments.

Interviewers will ask these particular questions in order to ascertain your adaptability skills, to assess your ability to adjust to unpredictable or changing environments at work— for example, when a new software, system, or other technology is introduced. In addition, interviewers wish to know how capable you are of taking on new tasks even if they aren't in your job description. By asking these types of questions, interviewers are trying to determine which of the applicants are more qualified than the others in terms of the following:

- dealing with unpredictable situations (e.g. a team member has quit)
- adjusting to changing circumstances (e.g. a client has modified their requests)
- helping out their fellow workers with embracing any switches that occur (e.g. when they need to begin following a new company policy)
- taking on new tasks (e.g. when their job requirements have increased)

However, there can also be some red flags for the interviewer if you are not careful with your answers that may cause the following concerns:

- **You are not open-minded.** People who stick to only what they already know and show reluctance to try non-traditional solutions aren't as likely to adapt to change.

- **You are afraid of the unknown.** If your company environment is a fast-paced one and employees are required to take on several tasks that go beyond their scope of responsibilities, they need to look for candidates who have no fear of learning new skills and taking risks.

- **You are nervous about changes.** Candidates who aren't able to stay calm with sudden changes aren't likely to have the ability to find effective and quick solutions to unexpected problems.

- **You are a negative individual.** Candidates who are in the habit of blaming others and are grumpy when they have to adapt to a change aren't as likely to be able to accept new circumstances.

- **You are not a team player.** Being able to adapt also means being able to adjust your working style for the sake of the team; interviewers value candidates who value collaboration and flexibility.

SAMPLE ANSWER to the question *"Describe a situation when you had to learn something new on the spot."*

Situation: *"I had a situation where I needed to learn new teaching methods. My first teaching job was at a school with a high level of discipline; one could spend hours lecturing and the students always paid attention. However, that changed with my most recent job, in which I had unruly students in every class."*

Task: *"Rather than blame the students, I decided to take on the responsibility of attempting to make the lessons more interesting and engaging."*

Action: *"In addition to applying new teaching methods, such as a flipped classroom or learning by playing, I also began to show the students documentaries and invite inspirational guests. From this, I managed to win most of the students over."*

Results: *"The students started paying attention because they began to enjoy the lessons and played an important part in them. Although it didn't work with everyone, it still worked with many, and I am glad that I made the decision to step outside of my comfort zone and learn something new."*

Possible questions on adaptability

- *Are you someone who can adapt to different work environments?*
- *What are some challenges you experience when starting a new job?*
- *Tell me about a time someone asked you to do something outside of your job description.*
- *How do you adjust to changes that you have no control over?*
- *How do you approach a new and unfamiliar task?*
- *How do you adjust your work style when working in a team?*

SAMPLE QUESTION #17

"Could you describe a situation when you used your communication skills?"

This is a question that is about building relationships, explaining processes, illuminating ideas, and sharing expectations, which are all vital working practices that can't take place without effective communication skills.

Employees, no matter what position they occupy in the company or their seniority level, will interact with clients, colleagues, customers, managers, partners, or team leaders every day, which is why good communication skills are crucial in the workplace. For example, a senior manager should have the ability to communicate tough decisions, as well as the ability to handle challenging situations and discussions at work. Customer service representatives, as another example, must appear to be empathetic, friendly, and genuine when they are speaking with unsatisfied customers.

Job interviews let potential employers evaluate and assess how the candidates communicate and how they handle certain situations; the questions can also focus on teamwork to see whether or not they can both convey and listen to messages effectively.

The interviewers evaluate candidates based on the following questions.

Are you someone who:

- is easy to get along with?
- can communicate effectively with different personalities?
- can respond adequately to situations that happen at work?
- is capable of adjusting to changing work environments?
- can assist their coworkers or team when it is required?
- is flexible in their approaches to situations at work?

There are several communication skills that the interviewers might be on the lookout for during the interview itself. Most of them are general in nature and are applicable to most work situations that could arise in your workplace. If you really want to stand out from your fellow applicants, you have to do your research to discover the exact communication skills that the employer values, such as confidence, emotional intelligence, empathy, friendliness, listening, nonverbal communication, open-mindedness, and/or respect.

When you answer communication interview questions, focus on the following key communication skills:

- active listening
- adjusting your communication styles to fit with different needs
- asking the correct questions to gain clarity
- encouraging feedback and questions from other people
- managing your emotions when you do communicate
- picking and organizing the correct information before talking
- understanding other people's viewpoints and demonstrating empathy

SAMPLE ANSWER to the question *"Could you describe a situation when you used your communication skills?"*

Situation: *"At my last job as a customer service representative, I dealt with many unsatisfied customers. However, one situation that comes to mind is a time when we had a customer who was upset that something had gone wrong with an online order. They had ordered several items to be delivered, but due to a glitch in the system, their credit card had been charged but the order had not gone through and their items were not delivered. "*

Task: *"I knew that I had to do everything in my power to satisfy the customer and make things right for them."*

Action: *"I communicated with my manager first about possible refund options before I began speaking with the customer and explained about the mistake that had been made. I apologized profusely and offered a partial refund of the delivery cost and half of* the order, as well as a 50% off coupon to use for their next purchase."

Result: *"The customer was placated with my suggestion and accepted my offer; they even left us five-star reviews on several different sites."*

Possible questions on communication

- *Tell me about a tough conversation you had to have with a team member.*
- *Give me an example of when you had to use your persuasiveness at work.*
- *Describe a time when you had to express your ideas in a meeting.*
- *Share a time when you had to present in front of a large audience.*
- *Tell me about a time when you had to rely on written communication to get your ideas across.*
- *Describe a time when you explained something complex to someone who had no clue about the topic.*

SAMPLE QUESTION #18

"Describe a time you had to meet a tight deadline."

This is a behavioral interview question regarding a candidate's time management; interviewers are usually eager to find candidates who can manage their own time in an effective manner. For an interviewer, this means that the candidate will need little direction if they are hired.

During an interview, the interviewer wants to discover how you manage your time and how you prioritize your decisions. For them, an employee who possesses the right skills in these areas has the ability to:

- adapt to changing situations reevaluate their priorities
- meet deadlines

- control their stress levels while dealing with multiple tasks
- manage their workload in an effective and efficient manner
- prioritize the most important projects first and put secondary tasks to the side
- use their time wisely while at the same time avoiding any possible distractions

Interviewers will look for candidates who demonstrate these skills, or even those who have the potential for growth in acquiring them. They want to know if you are able to deal with different tasks with different deadlines, and if you are capable of doing so without getting stressed or forgetting which tasks need to be done.

There are many specific elements that interviewers will look for; candidates who have great time management and prioritization skills do the following:

- **Use to-do lists.** People who are organized break down larger projects into smaller steps and use these kinds of lists, as well as reminders to make sure they stay on task. They are also more likely to complete their work inside set deadlines. Ensure that your answers include how you structure your approach to work and tasks to make sure that you can deliver what is needed on time.

- **Separate the urgent and important tasks.** During work, a lot of things are deemed important," but only some tasks are urgent and time-sensitive. Interviewers will look for candidates who understand the difference between tasks that are important and which are urgent, and be able to use that distinction to meet deadlines. Ergo, be sure that when the interviewer brings this category up, you are ready with an example of a time where you had to prioritize your tasks.

- **The ability to estimate the required effort, resources, and time for a project** is crucial in order to properly manage your time and task prioritization. The answers that you provide should include your strategies for evaluating and preparing a project in order to guarantee that you understand the requirements before you begin your work.

- **Don't hesitate to reevaluate their tasks.** In order to meet deadlines, employees must be able to identify any possible inefficiencies in their planning and workload. Once they've identified them, they need to figure out how to improve the processes. Be sure that your answers show that you are capable of reassessing your duties and that you successfully determined what works and what doesn't during times when this was required.

However, some answers can be seen as red flags to interviewers, so avoid the following responses:

- **Accepting missed deadlines.** While everyone misses a deadline sometimes, if you are giving an example of a time that happened to you, be clear that you are in fact aware that it is a problem and that it is something not typical to your character.

- **Not demonstrating awareness of your impact.** When you don't finish a task during a time constraint, it can affect the company as a whole. The responses to questions about time management should demonstrate that you understand that the actions you take, and the ones that you don't take, affect other people.

- **Being imbalanced.** Any good employer will want to avoid employee burnout; if you are too focused on your work and don't give yourself time to wind down in your personal life, that is a concern for potential employers.

SAMPLE ANSWER to the question *"Describe a time you had to meet a tight deadline."*

Situation: *"In my previous employment as a research assistant, I often assisted in preparing presentations and proposal submissions. This was a job with tight submission deadlines that required proper time management and communication to be successful."*

Task: *"One of my tasks was to prepare research presentations on complex topics for scientific meetings, which required coordination with researchers, data gathering, and creating visuals such as* *charts and graphs."*

Action: *"To ensure that the deadlines were met, I used project management tools and wrote to-do lists to track my tasks. I set aside specific amounts of time for the parts that I knew would take a longer time to complete, such as data collection and analysis."*

Result: *"I learned how to optimize my time, which helped me to meet deadlines faster and earn more favorable feedback on the information that I presented."*

Possible questions on time management

- *Give me an example of how you prioritize your projects.*
- *Tell me how you limit distractions during your work.*
- *Tell me about a time when you were late to complete a task, or you missed a deadline.*
- *Tell me about a time when you had an unexpected event that required you to adjust your priorities.*
- *Describe a time when you had to organize your workload having multiple projects at the same time*
- *Describe a long-term project that you kept on track. How did you keep everything moving?*

SAMPLE QUESTION #19

"When have you had to develop a creative approach to problem-solving to get the job done?"

Creativity refers to the act of creating new and imaginative ideas. Being creative is often beneficial to solving problems and communicating with others at work. Creative thinking can involve bringing the following to a workplace:

- a new approach to a problem
- a resolution to a conflict between employees
- a new result from a set of data
- a previously untried approach to earn company revenue
- a new product or product feature

During job interviews, the interviewer is looking for candidates who possess the following creative thinking skills:

- **Open-mindedness.** If you want to be engaging then you need to be open-minded; innovation doesn't just mean coming up with new ideas, but also tackling existing ideas in a different way. Being open-minded means considering alternative approaches to solving problems while pushing aside any assumptions or biases. You need to look at things from different perspectives.

- **Analytical thinking.** This gives you the ability to analyze and understand a situation that you've found yourself in. In order to start thinking of creative solutions to a challenge or problem, you have to understand what it actually is that needs to be worked on. Analytical skills help you to analyze things closely in order to fully understand their meanings. Regardless of whether you are working on strategies, processes, or even data sets, you have to have the ability to analyze information to solve problems and to make decisions.

- **Problem-solving skills.** These kinds of skills help you to determine what caused a challenge or problem and look for effective solutions to solve them. Key problem-solving skills include active listening, analysis, decision-making, and researching. Ergo, it is important in an interview to highlight not only your ability to think creatively, but also to solve challenges and problems.

- **Communication.** As soon as you've identified a problem and have come up with a creative solution to solve it, it is important that you have the know-how to communicate it to other people, whether it be a colleague, client, or supervisor. Communicating clearly is crucial in the workplace and helps to reduce confusion, which in turn makes the implementation of ideas easier and more efficient. Active listening is part of having great communication skills, and it is through this particular skill that you are able to process ideas and concepts effectively. When you ask the right questions and have an in-depth understanding of problems and challenges, you can come up with unique approaches to address issues.

- ***Organizational skills.*** This is a skill that references your ability to stay focused on multiple tasks by using your energy, strengths, and time effectively and efficiently in order to reach the desired outcome. Organizational skills are a big part of channeling your creative thoughts into plans of action. Having the ability to structure your ideas into actionable plans which include deadlines and goals is crucial.

SAMPLE ANSWER to the question *"When have you had to develop a creative approach to problem-solving to get the job done."*

Situation: *"At my previous position, I cannot recollect having to come up with a fair amount of creative solutions. We primarily worked with pre-set queries and, while there was some degree of creativity in regards to interpreting the data during analysis, I do not think a single solution stands out as particularly creative."*

Task: *"However, if I am faced with a challenge that can't be solved by traditional means, I do make it a goal to determine the exact issues that need to be addressed."*

Action: *"As I believe that unique problems need unique solutions, I will openly explore all the potential solutions regardless of whether or not they've been used in the past, sometimes even more than once, as I am aware that whatever I find may become the "go-to" solution in the future."*

Result: *"In my own experience, not being afraid of trying out new techniques to address any kind of obstacle has exponentially helped both the company and my own growth. I know that from this experience, I can come up with creative solutions when the situation needs one."*

Possible questions on creativity

- *When have you had to think outside of the box to solve a problem?*
- *Tell me about a business problem that you had to solve in a unique or innovative way. What was the outcome?*

- *Talk about a time when you presented a creative idea to your co-workers.*
- *Tell me how you go about encouraging ideas in others.*
- *Tell me about ideas you have created that benefited your current/former employer.*
- *What is the most creative project or idea that you have generated in a previous position? How was it received?*

SAMPLE QUESTION #20

"Give me an example of a time that accuracy was extremely important in your work."

This last example question of the chapter relates to attention to detail. For many professionals, such as developers, editors, and lawyers, accuracy is an important part of their day-to-day activities. Employees who are detail-oriented are of high value to employers because they produce excellent work and don't need a lot of supervision. Detail orientation is a transferable skill across most professions, and helps employees achieve their goals and generate better outcomes because of their commitment to creating works that are free of errors. Also, detail-oriented individuals often work more efficiently and are more prone to improving on their weaknesses without needing guidance or intervention.

All of these factors are appealing to employers and might result in higher-quality work that in the end supports the company's success. There are many ways to determine if you are a detail-oriented individual; people with a high level of this skill tend to:

- produce high-quality work with minimal errors
- provide information in a format that is useable and in a timely manner
- maintain checklists, notes, and schedules to ensure details aren't overlooked
- follow policies and procedures
- Interviewers use behavioral questions to assess a candidates'

analytical skills, such as their ability to organize, plan, and deal with errors, as well as their attention to detail.

When you are being interviewed for a position that is detail-oriented, you should be prepared to talk about the specifics in regards to your processes. Generic responses will be considered a red flag by interviewers, so they should be avoided.

SAMPLE ANSWER to the question *"Give me an example of a time that accuracy was extremely important in your work."*

Situation: *"At my last employment, one of my responsibilities was to provide a newsletter to our clients. This newsletter was important because it included vital dates and company statistics."*

Task: *"This information was critical to get right because it was a direct reflection of how the company was performing, so accuracy was very important."*

Action: *"In order to ensure accuracy, I took the time to review my work several times, asked my coworkers to look over my work, and requested feedback at every step I took."*

Result: *"The newsletters I put out were accurate with very few mistakes because of the feedback given to me by my coworkers. The company conveyed to me more than once how pleased they were with my work."*

Possible questions on attention to detail.

- *Can you describe a time when a co-worker made a mistake and you discovered it? How did you approach the situation?*
- *Do prefer to work with the "big picture" or the "details" of a situation? Give me an example of an experience that illustrates your preference.*
- *Have you ever found an error that wasn't obvious from the start?*
- *Tell me about a time when you made a mistake in your work. How did you find it and what did you to make it up?*

- *What do you do to verify that your work is accurate? Give me an example.*
- *Describe a time you identified an error made by your manager or a senior. How did you address it with them?*

CHAPTER 10

How to Distinguish Your Answers from Other Applicants'

I t doesn't need to be said that one might be overwhelmed by all of the information and examples that have been discussed thus far, especially considering how stressful job interviews already are and now one has to think about how they need to stand out from the crowd as well. While the 20 common questions from the previous chapter are meant to be helpful guidelines to answer behavioral questions, they are far from the exact answers that should be used, especially if your previous employment wasn't covered in one of the answers.

So how exactly should you distinguish yourself from the rest of the pack? How can you make yourself so unique that an interviewer would seriously consider you for employment at their company? There are a few bits of information that will be covered in this chapter that will help you, the first of which is the top five tips that will help you get the most out of using the STAR method.

1. Be specific

Using the STAR method means that you should never be vague, and this goes hand in hand with being prepared. Before your interview, you should have already identified the qualities and skills that the company is looking for. Be sure that your stories specifically target what is in the job advertisement, and don't forget that you need to emphasize the necessary behaviors that the interviewer is interested in. Being too general will not only make it hard for the interviewer to get a feel for you, it will also lessen your story's impact.

2. Be quantitative

This is an important part of your answers, as interviewers love numbers. You should include confirmable results to back up your stories. How much did you increase company revenue? By what percentage did you make your team more efficient? When possible, back up your successes with the numbers and hard facts.

3. Be concise

While your stories need to be targeted, they also can't be too long; you need to keep them short and sweet. That means no adding extra information and/or boring details that aren't relevant to the question asked. By doing this, your answers will have more of an impact, especially if you touch on all the points of the STAR method.

4. Be honest

As much as you want to shine your brilliant light to the interviewer, never tell them a story that isn't 100% true. Lying doesn't just damage your credibility in the future if your dishonesty is discovered, it also causes others to question their own ability to trust you in general—and there isn't a person out there who wants to hire someone they can't trust.

5. Be focused on your own actions and achievements

Always show off your experiences in past employment and your qualifications without mentioning your teammates or employers.

As important as teamwork is, what potential employers really want to know is if you are capable of working efficiently and contributing to the company on your own two feet.

The Most Common Mistakes to Avoid

As everyone knows, simply getting to the interview point is hard; hiring managers have to go through many applications just to choose you as someone they want an audience with. But, even after you land the interview, don't make the mistake of assuming the job is yours; now you have to make a great first impression.There are many, many mistakes that can be made at this stage that will blow your chance of being hired.

So, below are some common mistakes that you need to avoid, divided into two categories: general mistakes and the mistakes that are made during the interview itself.

General Mistakes

1. ***Arriving either too late or too early.*** You should arrive at your interview either on time or only slightly early,ten to fifteen minutes at the most, so the interviewer can complete whatever work they need to feel prepared to talk to you. Being on time demonstrates that you are punctual and that you value others' time.

2. ***Wearing inappropriate attire.*** Always look your most professional at an interview, even if the company you applied to has a casual dress code. Looking professional demonstrates to potential employers that you are serious about the job.

3. ***Cell phone use.*** Instead of looking at your phone while you wait for the interview to begin, look over your resume in order to prepare. Better yet, turn your phone completely off; not only will it help you to stay focused and distraction-free, it will also prevent any interruptions from calls or texts.

4. ***Not being sure of resume facts***. You really need to get to know the details of your resume before you are interviewed, especially things like important dates, prior employment, and

previous tasks. Make sure to bring a printed copy of your resume in a professional-looking folder so you can keep rereading it while you are waiting. You can even bring an extra copy for the interviewer in case they request one.

5. *Interrupting the interviewer.* No matter what, never interrupt your interviewer for any reason; not only is it rude, but it can also leave them with a negative impression. If you don't understand the question being asked, wait until they've finished speaking and ask for clarification. If you thought of a perfect response to their question before they've finished speaking, still wait until the end. If you do forget and blurt out words, apologize and again wait until they've finished.

6. *Speaking poorly of past employers.* This book already touched on the fact that one should never speak badly of previous employers, but it is something that can never be overly emphasized. Instead, share your learning experiences by focusing on the skills you've developed and your plans for the new role. Spin any negative answers into positive ones to demonstrate that you possess conflict resolution skills and are able to work well with others.

7. *Asking overly personal questions.* Any questions that you have to ask the interviewer should be appropriate and professional; save the personal details for later if you get the job. Keep the questions geared toward the company and role in question; for example, what the company culture is like, what the company's important goals are at present, and who you would directly report to.

8. *Not following up.* After the interview, either send the interviewer an email or properly written handwritten note, thanking them for their time and reminding them of your interest in the role. Share something about the role that has you excited for the opportunity and also include something that you learned during the interview to show them that you were paying attention. More details about the after-interview process will be covered in *Chapter 15.*

Behavioral Interview Mistakes

1. ***Being unprepared.*** When the interviewer can see that you didn't prepare for the interview, you are much less likely to be hired. You will show your unpreparedness by failing to give specific examples related to the question, giving answers that are too general or vague, or by rambling on and preventing the interviewer from asking further questions.

2. ***Not answering a question correctly.*** This goes along with being unprepared; telling a story that isn't related to the question causes the interviewer to believe that you lack focus and aren't attentive to detail, which are two qualities that every good candidate should possess.

3. ***Casting a negative light on your performances.*** The mindset of "the whole truth and nothing but the truth" doesn't have a place in interviews, not just because of how much rambling could take place, but also because overly honest answers about past poor performances don't shine a positive light on you as a potential employee. Stick to answers that are both honest and make you look good.

Tricks to Show the Best of Your Personality

However, it is not just telling stories that are true and accurate and using the STAR method that help you stand out from other candidates for the role; what also helps to set you apart is to allow your personality to come through during the interview. While being professional during an interview is extremely important, letting the interviewer see your personality can impact whether or not you get hired.

Being professional doesn't mean that you have to "fake" a personality or behave like a robot; at the same time, however, you should avoid talking to the interviewer like you are close friends or family. They are looking to see if you are a good fit for the company culture and if you do in fact connect. So, how do you toe the line between being friendly and being too friendly? Below are some tricks to show off your personality without getting too personal.

- **Ask certain questions.** You can reveal to the interviewer who you are as a person by asking certain types of questions that reveal what interests, passions, and values you possess. In addition, asking questions creates more conversation between you and your interviewer, which can make both of you feel more relaxed and easy with each other. As a bonus, when you ask the questions that you really want the answers to, you will get to learn more about the role and how well you will get along with the interviewer and fit in at the company. More about questions asked will be covered in Chapter 12.

- **Be friendly and engaging.** Greet every new person you meet with a warm smile and a friendly handshake, because first impressions are always important. Always show confidence right away; stand tall to demonstrate this. When you are answering the questions, you need to be animated in order to gain a connection with the interviewer. Be creative when expressing ideas and you'll come across as a well-rounded person, and if you look excited about what you're talking about, they will be too.

- **Don't sound negative.** When you are answering questions, you should never focus on the negative aspects of your story; instead, focus on the positive ones, such as the lessons that you've learned, the good experiences you've had, and your planned contributions to the company. Also talk about what excites and motivates you about your potential future role.

- **Don't be afraid to show off your sense of humor.** Showing humor is fine, as long as you don't come across as trying too hard. It's a delicate balance for sure, but if you remember to be charming and laugh at yourself or a funny comment that your interviewer makes then you are set. Just avoid jokes that are inappropriate or off-color, and don't use sarcasm either; if you're an edgy person, this isn't the time to show it.

- **Be mindful of your body language.** After the first greetings, you should continue to look confident to everyone that you meet, interviewer or otherwise. Don't allow your posture to slouch, sit and stand straight, and do your best to avoid any nervous habits that you may possess, whether it be finger tapping or another visible tic that makes you look unprepared. Another thing you shouldn't do is to cross your arms, as it makes you appear unfriendly; stay calm and still with a positive posture to show that you are confident and open. More details will be covered below.

Body Language

Our body language, also known as nonverbal communication, reveals our inner thoughts and feelings to others without having to say a word. If you say one thing to the interviewer but your nonverbal cues are telling them something completely different, they will notice and may have second thoughts about your suitability as a candidate.

What is body language? Body language, as the name implies, is how our bodies act physically as a reflection of our inner selves. Actions that make up our nonverbal communication can include things like gestures (such as pointing), facial expressions, touching, eye contact, and actions such as sitting, standing, walking, etc. They convey our true intentions.

Positive and Negative Body Language

Positive body language sends interviewers the correct message about yourself as a person. Below is how you can show the interviewer that you are a great candidate using your body language, as well as the kinds of negative body language that you need to be careful about.

- *Appropriate interview wear.* While it's true that your initial greeting helps make a great first impression, the true first impression comes from how you're dressed. You need to research what is considered appropriate dress for your industry; while you may not necessarily need to come in a suit, you also shouldn't dress in shorts and sandals, even if the atmosphere is casual. Dressing in a way that is perceived as "serious" shows that you are serious about the job.

- **Sit and stand up straight.** This includes while you are in the waiting room and as you walk into the interview room. Do not slouch or lean back, which will convey that you are either unprofessional or are not taking the interview seriously; sitting up and even leaning forward a little demonstrates your interest. You should also keep your feet planted on the ground; try not to cross your legs, as they may fall asleep and cause you to switch positions, which could be interpreted as fidgeting. You don't need to be a statue, but you should remain relatively still.

- **Maintain eye contact.** Keeping eye contact with the interviewer shows them that you're paying attention and listening to what they are saying. That being said, you should still break eye contact occasionally, as staring intently into their eyes the entire time may make them feel uncomfortable.

- **Be mindful of hand motions**. Using our hands while we talk is normal, but you have to be extra-vigilant when it comes to your hand gestures during an interview. Don't be motionless, as keeping your hands still may lead to awkwardness in your appearance, but keep movements small and close to you. Avoid gestures such as pointing or punching as they come off as aggressive. If you have trouble with that, fold your hands and arms into your lap, keep them on the chairs' arms, or have a pen and notepad to take notes during the interview. In addition, don't allow any gestures to become so enthusiastic that they take away from your words.

One last piece of advice for you is to practice, practice, practice, either in front of a mirror or a trusted associate of yours. Allowing your body to "gear up" and get used to gestures that may be unfamiliar to you will help you appear more natural and relaxed in the interview.

CHAPTER 11

Follow-Up Questions

While behavioral interviews are structured, that doesn't mean they aren't flexible. Whoever is doing the interview has to ask probing questions to get deep into the candidate's answers, and are based upon both verbal and nonverbal language. Behavioral questions mainly create three to four probing questions centered on the applicant's initial answer.

Probing questions are also known as follow-up questions, and are asked of applicants when:

- initial answers are unclear, obscure, imprecise, or don't even fully answer the "lead" question.
- the interviewee's voice changes dramatically or their wording becomes negative.
- the interviewee looks like they are having a hard time forming an answer or takes a lot of pauses.

In such cases, your answers can be hard for the interviewer to interpret, and may not allow the interviewer to pinpoint your role in a specific example of your previous behavior. These types of responses are referred to as **"false STARs,"** they are mainly unclear statements regarding feelings and opinions or "what if" scenarios of what a candidate "would do." The most common causes are:

- **Feeling as fact.** The interviewers will keep an eye out for statements involving feelings or opinions. Examples include: *"I am great at thinking ahead," "I felt that I was the best supervisor and deserved to be compensated for this,"* and *"I showed a lot of initiative when I was asked to solve a problem."*

- **Using "we" in your answers.** If you use "we" when giving an example of being a team player, your interviewer may ask for more detail to understand your part in a situation. For example, *"What was your specific role on your team?"* The incorrect way to answer is *"We developed the system software;"* the correct way to answer is *"I helped with the development of the system software."*

- **The "would haves."** Also avoid using hypothetical scenarios in your answers. For example, *"I would have achieved the target sales,"* and *"In this situation, I would have spoken to my supervisor."*

It should be noted that probing questions are not created before a behavioral interview takes place; they are thought up on the spot based on how the candidate answers the lead questions. These kinds of questions are dependent on the interviewer having active listening and observation skills, which are needed as the interviewee speaks about their experience and past behavior. The questions should be open-ended and shouldn't prompt an applicant toward a certain response. Below are some examples:

- *"I'm not quite sure I understood. Could you please tell me more about that?"*

- *"I'm not certain what you mean by... Could you give me some examples?"*

- *"You mentioned... Could you tell me more about that? What stands out in your mind about that?"*

- *"This is what I thought I heard... Did I understand you correctly?"*

- *"Can you give me an example of...?"*
- *"You just told me about... I'd also like to know about..."*

If the individual conducting the interview likes your answer, yet would still like further information from you, excellent probing questions might include, *"How did you know to do that?"* or *"Where did you learn that technique?"*

The good news for you is that your answers to these follow-up questions don't have to adhere to the STAR format; instead, think of these questions like a conversation.

Good preparation for the behavioral interview process is essential, as already established. This preparation will likely allow you to provide the interviewer with most of the necessary information in your initial responses, thus avoiding the need to ask you a lot of these additional probing questions.

CHAPTER 12
Importance of Asking Questions

W hen the job interview is coming to a close, you may feel a sense of relief, but it is short-lived when the interviewer asks, *"Do you have any questions?"*

Interviewers will expect all of their candidates to have at least a couple of questions for them; if they don't, it's considered a red flag. That's because not asking questions of your own makes you look unprepared and/or uninterested, so you need to take the time beforehand to prepare questions of your own to ask the interviewer. It's not just about getting a job; you're also interviewing the employer to determine if the company and the position are right for you. The best questions to ask don't just give you the information that you require, but also put you in a positive light. There are some other things to bear in mind when creating your own list of questions.

- **Don't use 'yes' or 'no' questions:** The majority of the questions with a 'yes', 'no' or another kind of one-word answer are more than likely to be answered just by looking on the company website. Stick with questions that will create a conversation between yourself and the interviewer.

- **Only one question at a time:** Try not to use multi-part questions; those will overwhelm the interviewer. Every question should have a specific point.

- **Don't use 'me' questions:** These kinds of questions put you ahead of the interviewer; for example, questions about work hours, salary, and vacation time, among others. During an interview, you are trying to show the employer that you can be a benefit to the company, not the other way around. Only once you are offered a role should you ask what benefits you will receive as an employee.

- **Questions about multiple topics:** Try not to ask questions that focus on a single subject; for example, if you ask only about workload or hours, the interviewer might think that you aren't as hardworking as your previous answers claimed. Ask questions that cover a vast number of topics to show that you are curious and interested in all parts of the position.

- **Don't ask questions that are too personal:** As important as it is to have a good rapport with your interviewer, avoid asking personal questions that aren't public information. For example, if you noticed a work-related award on their desk, you can ask about it; but steer clear of really personal questions such as family, gender, etc.

Best Questions to Ask

Questions that are fine to ask can be categorized into several groups, which will be defined more throughout the chapter. The categories are as follows:

- Questions regarding the position
- Questions regarding the company
- Questions meant to impress the interviewer
- Questions regarding challenges, competition, and struggles

- Questions regarding opportunities and the future
- Closing questions

But how many questions do you ask an interviewer? At least two are recommended; one feels only somewhat less irresponsible than not asking any at all, and two or more make you look prepared and quite interested and curious about your employment.

Questions Regarding the Position

Before you ask questions that revolve around "the bigger picture," you need to have a strong understanding of what your role entails. Here are some common questions regarding the position:

- *What are the main responsibilities of the position?*
- *How would you describe the daily routine of this position?*
- *What is the induction process for new hires?*
- *How many people will I be working with?*
- *How much am I expected to accomplish in my first month/year in the role?*
- *Do you expect the position's responsibilities to change in the near future?*
- *What are the biggest obstacles that an individual in this role would face?*
- *What are the projects that need swift attention right now?*
- *What else outside of the description can you tell me about this job?*
- *Would the position require me to travel?*

If you understand the intricacies of your position and role, you can then begin asking the bigger and more generalized questions.

Questions Regarding the Company

You should demonstrate to the interviewer that you are a team player who would be proud to be a company member. Some of the examples of questions that show that you are interested in the company include:

- *What is the work culture like here?*
- *What is your favorite office tradition?*
- *What are the prospects for growth?*
- *What does a work day look like here?*
- *Can you tell me what the team is like?*
- *How has the company changed over the last few years?*
- *What's the work environment like here, is it typically collective or independent?*
- *How would you describe the management style of the company?*
- *What do you/your employees like the most about working here?*
- *What kinds of things about the company aren't widely known?*

These kinds of questions show that you don't just think about yourself and how you can get work done, but that you are someone who cares about the success of the company as a whole.

Questions Meant to Impress the Interviewer

If you want to draw more attention to any of your impressive attributes, even though you've already mentioned them in your resume, you can ask something like this:

"I'm proud to have earned my degree in accounting; do you see me as being able to utilize these skills and knowledge in this role?"

Using this setup highlights your skills again in a way that doesn't make you look arrogant. Here are some further questions to ask that show you are even more impressive than just what your resume and cover letter say about you:

- *What would you consider the best accomplishments for a person in this position over the next year?*
- *How do employees receive feedback?*
- *What are the experiences and skills that you are looking for in this position?*

- *What attributes does one need in order to be truly successful in this role?*
- *Are there any important projects that I would need to start working on soon?*
- *How will my performance be evaluated?*
- *What kind of skills are missing from the team that you are looking to fill with a new member?*

These kinds of questions leave a strong impression on the interviewer; but don't ask questions where the possible answers are too broad. If you do have a broad question to ask, trim them down into multiple, small questions and ask them one at a time.

Questions Regarding Challenges, Competition, and Struggles

Asking about the company struggles will let you start a dialogue about how you can add value to the company by helping to fix them. In addition, asking about their competition and day-to-day challenges gives you insight into whether the position is a good fit for you. Below is a list of good questions to ask interviewers about the company's current challenges, competition, and struggles:

- *Which competitors/products/targets have you the most concerned?*
- *What are the biggest challenges of this role?*
- *What's the biggest challenge/change that the company/ department/industry has had to come up against recently?*
- *What area is the company currently focusing on as a whole?*
- *How many employees have left the company in the past year?*

These kinds of questions demonstrate that your mind is already in the role and in the game; this will not only impress your interviewers, but will also make it easier for you to imagine yourself in that role too.

Questions Regarding Opportunities and the Future

It's always a good thing to ask about the role's current responsibilities and/or the daily routine of the company, but don't forget to ask about future opportunities as well. You can also show that you are worth hiring and demonstrate that you care about the company and the role by asking how they develop or move forward. Here are some sample questions to ask at an interview's end about the company's future.

- *What are the opportunities for growth and advancement?*
- *Will there be opportunities for professional development?*
- *Is there a particular career path that someone in the position is expected to follow?*
- *How many people have recently joined the company?*
- *Where do you want the company to be in five years?*
- *What kinds of training programs are available to your employees?*
- *Is there an expectation to hire more people in the department in the next six months?*

When you demonstrate that you care about the company's future success, the interviewer will be quite happy; this is one of the best ways you can succeed in the interview.

Closing Questions

Before you leave the interview, ensure that the interviewer has all of the information they require and that you understand the next steps by asking the following questions:

- *Is there anything about my background that causes you concern about my fitness for this role?*
- *Is there something else I can provide you that would be helpful?*
- *Are there any final questions that you would like for me to answer?*
- *What is the length of your recruitment process?*

- *Would you like to know anything else about me that would help with your decision?*

- *If I am given a job offer, when would you like me to start?*

Don't forget to be relaxed and friendly, as you are more than likely going to be dealing with people who are friendly themselves, and they will respond to a positive outlook. Body language, as discussed in the previous chapter, is half of human communication; smile if you're happy, nod to acknowledge things, use hand gestures for point emphasis, and most of all, remember that you are going to do just fine!

Questions Not to Ask

When there are questions that can be asked, there will also be questions that you shouldn't ask. Some examples include:

- *Did I get the job?* (Shows impatience.)

- *What does the company do?* (That's why you research beforehand!)

- *If I get the job, when can I start to take vacations?* (Wait to gain the offer before you mention any prior commitments.)

- *If I get the job, can I change my schedule?* (If you have to figure out these kinds of logistics, don't bring it up now.)

- *How long would I have to wait for a promotion?* (Nailing the interview still doesn't guarantee that you are going to land the role, so you're basically jumping to the conclusion that you've already gotten the job.)

- *How often do you give out bonuses?* (They might think that you just want the job for the financial rewards and not the work itself.)

- *What perks and benefits can I expect?* (Like the question above, the interviewer might question your true motivation for applying for the position.)

- *When can I expect to hear back from you?* (Also implies that you believe that they are going to offer you the position. If they want you, they will contact you.)

- *When do you plan on making someone an offer for the job?* (A similar reason as above; you may think that not asking about yourself directly will fool them, but it won't.)

- *Can I see the break room?* (A question like this will imply that you are more interested in your break times than the actual work itself.)

In the additional material to this book there is an extended list of possible questions on what to ask and not to ask the interviewer.

CHAPTER 13
Video Interview Tips

Once, all interviews took place inside the building where you would be working should you land the job. However, the COVID-19 pandemic forced everything to change, as social distancing meant that the interviewer and the interviewee couldn't be in the same room together.Something had to change, but what? That's where technology stepped in and helped to establish a new breed of interview: the video interview. This meant the interviewee had to make further changes to how they are interviewed in addition to having the ability to answer the questions in the right ways.

This chapter will provide you with 12 tips that cover how you can set yourself up for a great video interview.

Tip #1: Arranging Your Background

When you are being interviewed on video, the interviewer is going to see everything that the camera picks up, including the background and how the background is set up; this will either impress or depress an interviewer. Never have a messy background, and keep it neutral; your best bet is a plain wall, but if you don't have that, then try to make it look professional by utilizing a bookshelf, some plants, or even a nice painting. In addition, don't sit right up against the wall; have a minimum of three feet between the wall and the back of your head to prevent a flattening-looking shot. Be sure that your background and shirt are not matching colors, as you will blend into the background,making it harder for you to be seen.

Tip #2: Mastering the Lighting

Having good lighting will help to make you look great. Lighting can be a tricky thing to set up in your home, but there are a few ways that you can make it work for you. First, try to use natural lighting if possible; if you have light above you from a window, that's great. Try to avoid light from fluorescent bulbs or similar; also try to avoid window light directly behind you or over your head. If need be, put two lights, such as from table lamps, diagonally in front of you, with one a little to the left and the other to the right. However, do not use too much lighting; you don't want to be in the dark, but too much light can cause glaring on eyeglasses.

Tip #3: Don't Sit Too Close or Too Far

In the same way that you wouldn't sit too close or too far from your interviewer when meeting them in real life, you don't want to be in an uncomfortable position in front of your computer. You need to make sure that you don't look too big or too small to the camera; sit in a position where there is some empty space above your head, and ensure that your shoulders and upper chest are visible.

Tip #4: Choose a Small Chair

Sitting in a small chair eliminates a couple of problems. Firstly, it prevents slouching, making you look more professional; secondly, a small chair doesn't take up screen space with you—just make sure it doesn't make noise when you move around.

Tip #5: Eliminate Distractions

Having kids and pets in your house is a fact of life; however, that doesn't mean that you should allow them to be around when your interview is taking place. If they aren't allowed to attend a live interview, then they shouldn't be allowed in a virtual one, either. Pick and choose anything that distracts both of the parties for the entirety of the interview. Also, turn off any electronics, notifications, etc., that can distract you; you can also put up a sign on the front door requesting that outsiders don't knock or ring the doorbell.

Tip #6: Dress to Impress

You need to dress for a video interview in the same way that you would dress for a live interview; however, there are a few extras that you need to consider for the camera. First, don't wear anything that has bright colors and/or patterns; instead, opt for softer colors. A tie needs to be a solid color without a pattern and if you wear glasses, the room lighting has to be positioned in a way that prevents glare. Also, dress from head to toe, even if only your upper half is showing; if you have to stand up for some reason, you want to give the interviewer the right kind of eyeful.

Tip #7: Make a "Cheat Sheet"

One advantage to having a video interview over a live one is that the camera can only show the interviewer so much, which can be helpful to you in regards to keeping cheat sheets or notes, so long as you're careful about it. Keep the notes small and short, and don't keep them in front of you; your best bet is to keep key information on Post-It Notes and stick them on top of the screen without blocking the camera the interviewer will never know about them.

Tip #8: Test Your Tech

One of the worst things that could happen to you is any part of your tech not working, but there are a few things that you can do to help with that. You should always check your internet connection, as that's the quickest way a video interview can fail. Make sure that your computer connects with both your camera and microphone and that your earbuds work. Also make sure that there are no programs running or downloading.

Tip #9: Have a Backup Plan

Sometimes even the most well-thought-out plans can fail, which is why having backup plans is crucial. In case of device failure, install a backup of the software used for the interview on a second device. Before the interview begins, ask the interviewer for a phone number to reach them in case video or audio stops working, in order to continue the interview over the phone or to reschedule. If loud noises interrupt, apologize and wait for the noise to subside; maybe even turn the microphone off. If someone interrupts, apologize and turn off the video and microphone to deal with them, making sure that the room is secure before resuming. Finally, if your earbuds don't work, have a second pair handy.

Tip #10: Be There Early

If you aren't walking into the interview building with only a couple minutes to spare, then you aren't going to do the same with a video interview. Boot up at least ten minutes before the interview to prepare yourself, open up the program, make sure that you don't have any of those silly filters on, and use the time to relax yourself and build up your confidence.

Tip #11: Have Good Eye Contact and Body Language

Having good eye contact with your interviewer means going against all instincts, which means not looking at the screen, but rather at the camera. That isn't easy, so practice beforehand. Remember, you must do this without slouching, so you can always put something underneath your laptop to raise it up if necessary. Your posture should also be the same as a live interview—back straight, feet on the ground, arms in your lap or on the desk, and smile and nod to indicate that you're listening.

Tip #12: Let the Other Person Finish Talking

Letting another person finish speaking is a little different during a video chat than during a live interview. Giving your response too quickly can cause the other person's mic to cut off, and internet lag doesn't always let you accurately gauge whether someone is finished talking or just pausing. Your best bet is to either wait a few seconds after they seem to have finished speaking, or mute your own mic and turn it back on when it's your turn to speak.

CHAPTER 14

Important Things to Do Before a Job Interview Invitation

Preparing for the job interview itself isn't the beginning of your journey toward landing a job; the beginning occurs before the interview itself, and entails having an excellent resume and cover letter to catch the interviewers' eyes. You can use the STAR method for this as well, which will be discussed throughout this chapter, starting with how to write your resume.

STAR Resume

The benefit of using the STAR method in a resume is tied into why you need a resume at all. Resumes give potential employers a good, yet quick sense of who you are and what kind of experiences you've gone through, as well as helping you to present your strengths and accomplishments. So, why the STAR method? Using the STAR method helps you to create a more exciting resume that demonstrates the following:

- a deep understanding of your work history, qualifications, and accomplishments
- your specific experiences that are relevant to the position that you're applying for, along with the practical experience that's required
- your potential value in a way that's clear and confident

The STAR method proves that you have what's necessary to achieve in the position, and it gives you a leg up over other jobseekers who submit generic resumes. Interviewers will be able to tell that you put both time and effort into personalizing your resume for the position.

So, how do you tailor a resume? When you read a job posting, you will notice that they include a list of responsibilities and qualifications that are either required or preferred. You take what's listed and use the same language/keywords in your resume to demonstrate that you can fulfill the role. It proves that you have what the employer is looking for, and that you have used the same skills before to create great results at work.

There are even more benefits to tailoring your resume using the STAR method. It can show how you align with the job, it shows that you are really interested in the job, it places emphasis on what the employer needs, and it can help you pass through those applicant tracking systems that are used by many employers nowadays. Below are the steps that you can take to create a powerful resume tailored to the job description.

Step 1. Review the Description

Carefully read over the description and write down or highlight any significant keywords that are related to skills; they might be words or phrases that look unique to the job or occur more than once throughout the posting. Then note the specific requirements, like the education, training, and years of experience that are necessary.

You should also note the order of the responsibilities listed, as the ones mentioned first might be higher priority for the employer. You will want to duplicate the priorities when you are organizing your resume; if they mention certain items first in the job description, you should mention those items first as well.

Step 2. Update Your Summary

As the summary section is at the top of your resume, it will be one of the first things that a hiring manager sees. If you have one, use it to demonstrate your most relevant accomplishments and skills based on your highlighted keywords. It is also recommended that you include the title of the job to which you are applying for, showing that this is a personalized resume.

Step 3. Customize Your Work History

This will be the next most visible section on your resume, so you should allow the hiring manager to immediately tell you that you have the necessary experience. If you have a long work history, this might mean that you have to downsize or remove any previous positions that do not align with what is required for the job; Or, if your most relevant jobs were further back, you can split this section in two: one section that details "industry experience" and one that details "other work" experience.

Using bulleted lists under each position is a great way to clearly show off your transferable skills and demonstrate your history of success. Here are step-by-step instructions to help out:

1. Determine five to seven skills that are the most relevant to the position

- e.g. Problem-Solving, Communication, Leadership, Research, Analytics

2. Identify your key accomplishments and skills used in each

- What did you build/create? What concepts/ideas did you develop?

- Did you direct people/projects?
- What problems have you solved? What challenges had been overcome?
- What were you most proud of in your previous job? Did you receive any promotions or awards/accommodations?

3. Using the STAR Method, choose which accomplishments show five to seven relevant skills; list the following for each of them.

- what you did (the situation or task)
- how you did it (the actions)
- the impact of the actions (the results)

4. Write out the bullet points in a way that shows the situation or task, the action, and the result of the accomplishment.

- Start each bullet point with action verbs.
- Choose the first words of every point carefully; begin with your relevant skill or impact.
- Get rid of any jargon that isn't relevant, but use the jargon that is.
- Quantify (#, %, $) the impact. Did the sales/profits increase? Did costs decrease? Was there time saved? Did you go beyond your goals? And if you did, by how much?
- Give context when quantifiable results can't be given. Think of the intended impact or results vs. last year or vs. your peers. Make mention of whether or not you received any kind of commendation.

Using Action Verbs

The majority of resumes sent out to potential employers contain words and phrases like "handled," "responsible for," and "tasked with." However, despite their commonality, they aren't helpful because they are passive words and don't show your actual accomplishments, and thus including them is a very easy way for your resume to be discarded. Using action verbs in your resume with bullet points shows what you can do and makes your resume stand out, helping you to land interviews. There are hundreds of action words that you can use; listed below is a small sample organized into categories based on the specific situations when the words can be used. More words are available in the additional materials of this book.

You increased something positive

- Accrue
- Bolster
- Enhance
- Generate
- Propel

You reduced something negative

- Curtail
- Diminish
- Eliminate
- Slash
- Trim

You communicated effectively with colleagues and customers

- Address
- Compose
- Illustrate
- Negotiate
- Relay

You managed projects or people

- Administer
- Coordinate
- Facilitate
- Govern
- Oversee

You took the initiative to get something done

- Endeavor
- Forecast
- Overhaul
- Spearhead
- Undertake

You lead people to success

- Appoint
- Enlighten
- Foster
- Guide
- Nurture

You organized something

- Compile
- Integrate
- Merge
- Officiate
- Standardize

You brought people together

- Collaborate
- Motivate
- Reconcile
- Support
- Unify

You achieved something incredible

- Accomplish
- Debut
- Exceed
- Revitalize
- Surpass

You created a new way of doing things

- Conceptualize
- Draft
- Engineer
- Formulate
- Launch

Using numbers

It is a good idea to use numbers in your resume as they can help demonstrate quantifiable accomplishments, as well as showing potential future employers that if they hire you, you can add value to their goals. Numbers in particular are even more useful if you are applying for positions in accounting, executive leadership, finance, and sales, because they are roles that typically involve money management, reaching quotas, and making impacts on the company. As for other positions, numbers can be used to demonstrate the size of the team that you led or the time spent on a project's completion.

There are different kinds of numbers that should be used; below are 15 examples:

- Number of new clients
- By how much the revenue was increased
- Retention of clients
- Website traffic
- Engagement of users
- Subscriptions
- Donations
- Student test scores
- Response times
- Budget management
- Number of referrals
- Awards won

- Staff size
- Retention of staff
- Audit findings

Below are a couple of sample bullet points:

- *Optimized and redesigned accounting software in 10 days* *(**task**) for working and communicating remotely (**action**). The new version of the software was helpful in successfully organizing more than 30 members of the accounting department (**result**).*

- *Led a 10-person team in the design and development (**action**) of a new technology project worth $12M (**situation**), and finished one week ahead of schedule with a savings of 8% of the budget (**result**).*

As you can see from these examples, the bullet points don't contain the STAR method in the exact order of the acronyms, nor are they in separate sentences, the way you would answer interview questions. It isn't necessary to follow those rules in your resume because you aren't doing the thorough, yet short storytelling that's needed during an interview, you are simply briefly showcasing your accomplishments.

Step 4. Update Your Skills Section

Your summary and work history might not include all of the most relevant skills you have, so add any that don't fit to your skills section. like those sections, list the most prioritized skills first using the job description keywords. Then, include any other relevant skills that show off the unique value that you bring to the position. Include any "preferred" skills as they might be optional, but can still help set you apart as a top candidate.

Step 5. Proofread Your Resume

Besides scanning for grammatical and spelling errors, look over your resume to make sure that you used all relevant keywords and phrases. Compare your summary section to the overall description and ensure that they match. Then see to it that each bullet point in your work history is relevant to the role's responsibilities and requirements. You can also ask a friend or colleague to review your resume and provide feedback.

STAR Resume

| Step 1 | Step 2 | Step 3 | Step 4 | Step 5 |

In addition to passing any applicant tracking system that they may be using, you want to make sure that your language is specific enough to catch the readers' attention; seeing words or phrases that are familiar will show them that you understand what they need and are able to perform the responsibilities that the role entails.

STAR Cover Letter

A cover letter (or rather a "covering letter") is a short letter about only a page long that explains why you are the best candidate for a job role and why you would like to work for the employer. While your resume also does that, the cover letter is the first chance for you to make a great impression, as well as providing a sample of your writing skills. Having a cover letter is important because it helps a potential employer connect the dots between what your qualifications are and what they want or need from you. While you know exactly why you're qualified for the role, a cover letter will help the employer understand this too. However, there are things that a cover letter is, and there are things that a cover isn't, as detailed below.

What a Cover Letter Is

- A chance to "make a case" for yourself regarding your fitness to potential employers so that they want to bring you in for an interview.

- An introduction to your application that targets the position specifically.
- An opportunity to make connections between the categories that employers want, such as your qualifications, skills, experience, and education.
- A sample of your writing skills.

What a Cover Letter Isn't

- An introduction to your application.
- A list of your accomplishments.
- A summary of your resume.
- Something that is written quickly and without much thought put into it.
- Not as important as your resume.
- Something that can be skipped; even if an employer doesn't request one, it is still strongly suggested that you write one.

Cover letters, like resumes, do follow a particular format in regards to how they are written.

Cover Letter General Structure

A cover letter is never more than a page long and is composed of three paragraphs. To remember this, think of them as a meal: the first paragraph is the appetizer, the second is the main course, and the final one is dessert. Each paragraph has to offer up to the employers a different piece of yourself, but keep them brief to stay within the one-page limit.

First paragraph

The first paragraph is the introduction, and is what is going to make the employers keep reading your letter. This is the paragraph where you state precisely who you are and explains why you are applying for the role. You also need to incorporate any research that you've done; this includes any employees that you have connected with via networking and informational interviewing. As this is the appetizer of the course, it has to be good, as it is a precursor to how good the meal is supposed to be. Hook the employer in to keep them reading so they want to know more about you.

Second paragraph

The second paragraph is the body of the letter and it also demonstrates to the potential employer what it is you have to offer them as an employee; it's the paragraph that allows them to connect the dots. In this paragraph, you "make your case" by drawing connections between the requirements of the job and your own attributes, experiences, and skills. Highlight one or two specific accomplishments that are not already included in your resume. If you are making a career switch, then you have to state, not plead, your case as to why you believe that you will still make an effective employee. Show them what you have to offer by describing the experiences and skills that make you a good match for the position as well as the qualities and attributes that make you a good fit, with examples. As this is the main course of the meal, it's the most memorable part the part where you will convince the reader that you are at least worth an interview.

Third paragraph

The closing paragraph is written to demonstrate what it is you want and how you are going to follow up; this is the part where you get the potential employer to take action. You are to reinstate your enthusiasm and interest in the job and recap what you can do for them and how they will benefit from having you. Also, make a specific request, such as scheduling an interview, and outline your follow-up; thank the reader for their time and consideration. Don't forget, as this is the dessert phase of the meal, to end on a great note to help land you an interview and make a lasting impression.

Additional Important Information

Below is some further information that should be remembered when writing a cover letter.

- Be very specific with your contact information.

- Always be formal; address the reader as Mr. or Ms. (which is always a safe title to say regardless of marital status); even if you know the individual well, it is always best to remain professional as that individual may send your letter and resume to someone that you aren't familiar with, such as their boss.

- If you have been networking and know who to address the letter to, that's great! If you don't know the name of the department leader, address the letter to "Dear Hiring Manager."

- And importantly, always tailor your letter to each job; just like with your resume, never go generic!

- In addition, use an 11 or 12-point font, make sure that the margins are at least an inch all around, aligned to the left, and use proper business formatting and spacing.

How STAR Fits In

So, where does the STAR method fit into a cover letter, if it is different from a resume? As already established, the STAR method is used to give (not too much) detail to your accomplishments; as discussed above, this is the role of the second paragraph therefore, the second paragraph is where the STAR method is used!

This is also where you have the most flexibility in regards to how the method is used. You can either use it in the order that you would during an interview, or present it in the way that you might a resume. What is important is that you use it appropriately as a boost to your credentials to help you get your foot in the door for the interview.

CHAPTER 15
After the Interview

You've made a great cover letter and resume, and you've landed that interview that you were hoping for and it has gone well; so that's the end, right? All you have to do is wait for that one phone call... Not quite that isn't the end of the story just yet! You still have things to do after the interview. While the interview may have felt daunting up until it was over with, the after-interview tasks may cause just as much anxiety, because following up with the interviewer might tip the scales in your favor, or leave you in the dust.

In this final chapter, you will learn the steps to take after your interview that will potentially increase your attractiveness to an employer. While the interview itself is used to screen potential new employees, what you do after the interview also makes an impact on your chance of getting the job. Following up after an interview allows you to present yourself as a professional, keeps your name fresh in the interviewer's mind, and it shows eagerness for the job.

- **Ask for next steps and contact information.** When an interview is wrapping up, it's important to get the contact information of the hiring manager and ask about the next steps; this can result in finding out when they plan to make their decision Instead of asking directly how long they think they need to make a decision, ask if there will be a second interview, and if there is, when they will be notifying the candidates that are moving on.

- **Assess your interview performance.** To assess your own performance, write down the questions that you remember answering and how you answered them; also include what you didn't say but that you wish you had. You might be able to work some of them into the follow-up; the point is to identify issues and why they occurred, which can help you in future interviews.

- **Write down anything that you want to remember.** If there is anything else that you want to remember in addition to the above, write it down too. For example, insight into the office environment, or the names of employees you met, or anything that you learned about the interviewers that could be relevant should you get a second interview.

- **Send a thank-you note to the hiring manager.** Sending out a thank you note within 24 hours of the interview is a particularly important post-interview step to take. For some industries, a more formal note such as a handwritten thank-you card might be best. Research the best way to say thank you, and don't forget to convey gratitude to the individual who took the time to interview you.

- **Connect on social media business networking sites**. If you use any social media that focuses on business networking, see if you are able to connect with your interviewer after the interview; if they accept, it could be a sign that they are interested in getting to know you better, and is an important part of growing your personal network. Even if in the end you get a job with a different company, growing your network is still helpful to remain aware of future opportunities.

- **Send supporting documents.** If there is a request for supporting documents, then those are sent post-interview; these could include a reference page, written assessment, or even consent forms for various background checks as part of the pre-screening process. Getting these to an interviewer is definitely a top priority.

- **Contact your references.** If you have submitted references to your potential employer, you should let them know that someone might contact them. It is considered proper to only submit references of people who have consented to you using them. If you think they will be called, notify them in advance.

- **Get comfortable with waiting.** In addition to all of the above, you can spend your waiting time picking up new skills and preparing for your next interview. If you have connections with people in the company, see if they can offer more insight or speak to the hiring manager on your behalf. Keep calm and only call or email as per the hiring manager's preferences.

Follow-Up Emails

In general, there are two kinds of follow-up emails that you can send after an interview: the "thank you" email mentioned above, and a "check-in" email to stay in touch for networking purposes.If you don't hear back in a timely manner, you may send a second follow-up email.

Sometimes only the initial thank-you note is needed before you receive an official response, but there are times when weeks pass before you hear back from someone. Below are the best ways to write follow up emails after an interview.

Start by thanking your interviewer for their time. Ensure that you highlight the ways that your talents are aligned with the position; go back to your notes from the interview and the job description to carefully choose words or takeaways from your conversation that will stick with the reader. Again, show your interest in the position and your belief that you're right for the job. Here is a further step-by-step guide for writing a follow-up email:

1. Start by choosing the right subject line. The best subject lines are clear and show your appreciation for your interviewer's time. They include the following: *"Thank you for your time, [interviewer's name]," "Thank you for the opportunity,"* and *"I appreciate your time and advice."*

2. Open the first paragraph with a thank-you. Mention the specific job title, thank your interviewer for their time, and again express your interest in the position and company.

3. Talk about interests, goals, and experience. In the second paragraph, note the company name, in addition a conversation point or goal that appeared to be important to your interviewer and connect it with your experience and interests. Be as specific as possible while being short and to the point.

4. Set yourself apart. Close your email with a summary statement that highlights what puts you in a different category as a candidate and what you will bring to the job. Invite them to ask you any further questions and close off by saying that you're looking forward to hearing from them.

5. End with signature and contact information. Finish the email by including your signature and contact information; pick a professional yet friendly closing, like *"best," "sincerely,"* or *"thank you."*

Longer emails will give you the opportunity to explain your skills in detail, although you still need to keep it relatively short; this is what is appropriate after an in-person interview or other meaningful interactions during the hiring process.

Here are some additional follow-up tips you might consider when writing your own:

- If there's something that you forgot or wanted to elaborate on from the interview, this is a good time to mention it.

- Begin with the interviewer's name. Use their first name if you are on a first-name basis; if not, then use both their first and last names.

- Be sure to choose a length that is appropriate to your type of interview, the ones that are concise are often more appropriate.

- Always carefully proofread before you send. Like with everything else you send out to potential employers, give your follow-up a final edit before you let it go out.

- When you close your letter, make sure that you include your name and contact information, such as your phone number and email address.

If you haven't heard back from a potential employer after the interview or after your follow-up note, you can send an email that "checks in" after about a two-week period. Keep it concise, like your follow-up email; you need to show that you are still interested and are looking for more information, but without looking overeager. Read over the following tips:

- Include the job title you interviewed for in the subject line.

- The email should be sent to the recruiter, as they are likely the ones who are up-to-date on the hiring process.

- Keep it to one paragraph; show your interest in the job and explain that you are looking for an update. Offer to provide additional information at their request and sign off with a thank-you.

Conclusion

And now, you've come to the end of this book, and you've learned how you can make yourself stand out from other candidates in the workforce. You've learned that it is important to use the STAR method to distinguish yourself in an interview setting. You know how to show potential employers that you should be considered an asset for their company, and that you can add value to their future by demonstrating all of the good that you have done in the past.

The key takeaways that you should have gained from this book are as follows:

- The job description is essentially your Bible, as it is where you'll find all of the qualities that your future employer wants you to possess.
- To remember your situations from past job and non-job-related experiences during a behavioral interview.
- How to focus on your actions and contributions.
- Not to forget to tell the truth and not hesitate to ask for more time if it is needed.

- How to provide concrete examples with verifiable results.
- The kinds of questions that you should be prepared to ask the interviewer.
- How to follow up after the interview.

Regardless of what stage of your life you have decided to read this book, whether you are an experienced worker looking for a career change or fresh out of a higher educational institute looking for opportunities, you can benefit from the information that you have found in this book. You may have felt a little intimidated by the prospect of having to learn all of this new information, or at the very least, an update to information that you already knew.

While the STAR method requires a little finesse and practice to master, there's no doubt that it will help you succeed in finding gainful employment, no matter what stage you are at in your life. However, using STAR is only part of landing a great job, even if it is a big part; you also learned crucial techniques regarding how else to conduct yourself during the interview itself, including your body language, how to answer certain questions, and the kinds of questions that you might want to ask. Just have faith in yourself and practice, and you will land that job.

Happy job hunting!

Useful Extras

Thank you for choosing this guide on how to prepare for a behavioral interview. I sincerely hope it has been useful for you and you have enjoyed it. As a way of saying thanks for your purchase, I would like to share with you some complementary materials that will be quite helpful in preparing for your next STAR interview

You'll get the following extras:

1. *STAR Interview Practice Worksheet*
2. *400+ Popular Competency Based Behavioral Interview Questions*
3. *380+ Action Verbs*
4. *150+ Essential Soft Skills*
5. *230+ Powerful Adjectives*
6. *120+ Best Questions to Ask (and Not to Ask) an Interviewer*

You can download these extras by scanning the QR-code below

Feedback from awesome readers like you helps prospective readers feel confident about their choice of this book and I'd very much appreciate it if you would let me know what you think about this guide and leave a review.

Thank you!

Sincerely,

Martha Gage

References

1. "How to answer interview questions with the STAR method",
https://resume.io/blog/star-method
2. "The STAR Method: The Secret to Acing Your Next Job Interview",
https://www.themuse.com/advice/star-interview-method
3. "Everything You Need to Know About Answering Behavioral Interview Questions",
https://www.themuse.com/advice/behavioral-interview-questions-answers-examples
4. "60+ Behavioral interview questions – tips and examples",
https://resume.io/blog/behavioral-interview-questions
5. "How to Use the STAR Interview Response Method",
https://www.thebalancecareers.com/what-is-the-star-interview-response-technique-2061629
6. "How to Prepare for a Behavioral Job Interview",
https://www.thebalancecareers.com/behavioral-job-interviews-2058575
7. "Competency-Based Interview Questions",
https://www.thebalancecareers.com/competency-based-interview-questions-2061195
8. "10 Common Behavioral Interview Questions",
https://www.thebalancecareers.com/top-behavioral-interview-questions-2059618
9. "Behavioral Interviewing Techniques and Strategies",
https://www.thebalancecareers.com/behavioral-interview-techniques-and-strategies-2059621
10. "How To Use the STAR Interview Response Technique",
https://www.indeed.com/career-advice/interviewing/how-to-use-the-star-interview-response-technique
11. "7 Sample Behavioral Interview Questions and Answers",
https://www.indeed.com/career-advice/interviewing/behavioral-interview-questions
12. "Interview like a STAR and make the most of your stories",
https://www.betterup.com/blog/star-interview-method
13. "How to Use STAR Method Technique for Interview Questions",
https://zety.com/blog/star-method-interview
14. "40+ Common Behavioral Interview Questions & Answers",
https://zety.com/blog/behavioral-interview-questions
15. "19+ STAR Interview Questions- Complete List",
https://novoresume.com/career-blog/star-interview-questions
16. "How To Master the STAR Method For Interview Questions",
https://theinterviewguys.com/star-method/
17. "STAR Interview Method: Definition, Tips, and Examples",
https://www.cakeresume.com/resources/star-interview-method
18. "How to prepare for a behavioral/soft skills interview? ",
https://towardsdatascience.com/how-to-prepare-for-a-behavioral-soft-skills-interview-cheat-sheet-9347aaeaef82
19. "41 Behavioural Interview Questions You Must Know (Best Answers Included) ",
https://www.themartec.com/insidelook/behavioral-interview-questions
20. "Behavioral Interviewing",
https://eddy.com/hr-encyclopedia/behavioral-interviewing/

21. "What Is a Behavioral Interview? And How to Prepare for One",
https://www.topinterview.com/interview-advice/rock-behavioral-based-interview
22. "Everything You Need to Know About Behavioral Interviews",
https://www.careermatch.com/job-prep/interviews/behavioral-interviews/
23. "How to Prepare for a Behavioral Interview",
https://www.glassdoor.com/blog/guide/how-to-prepare-for-a-behavioral-interview/
24. "How To Prepare for a Behavioral Interview",
https://www.indeed.com/career-advice/interviewing/how-to-prepare-for-a-behavioral-interview
25. "How to Ace Interviews with the STAR Method [9+ Examples] ",
https://novoresume.com/career-blog/interview-star-method
26. "Common Behavioral Interview Questions with Answers",
https://www.interviewkickstart.com/career-advice/common-behavioral-interview-questions-answers
27. "The STAR Method Interview Questions + Answers & Examples (2022 Update) ",
https://www.interviewgold.com/advice/the-star-method-to-answer-questions/
28. "Ultimate STAR Method Guide to Answering Behavioral Interview Questions",
https://www.workstream.us/blog/ultimate-star-method-answering-guide
29. "20+ STAR Interview Questions & Best Answers",
https://www.algrim.co/451-star-interview-questions
30. "Behavioral Interview Questions And Answers 101 (+ Example Answers) ",
https://theinterviewguys.com/behavioral-interview-questions-and-answers-101/
31. "How to Use the STAR Method for Interview Questions",
https://www.careermatch.com/job-prep/interviews/star-method-interview-questions/
32. "Use the STAR Method to Shine in Your Interview",
https://www.flexjobs.com/blog/post/sar-method-answering-job-interview-questions-v2/
33. "What is the Star Method and why it will help you ace your next interview",
https://www.theladders.com/career-advice/what-is-the-star-method-and-why-it-will-help-you-ace-your-next-interview
34. "STAR Method: A Model Approach to Nail Your Next Interview",
https://www.mindtools.com/pages/article/STAR-method.htm
35. "STAR Technique/Approach: Applicant Handout",
https://www.gov.nt.ca/careers/sites/careers/files/resources/x_star_-_applicant_handout_-_updated_november_1_2017.pdf
36. "The Most Powerful Words to Use During Your Interview",
https://www.thebalancecareers.com/powerful-words-for-job-interviews-4123781
37. "Strong Words to Use in an Interview",
https://www.glassdoor.com/blog/guide/words-to-use-in-an-interview/
38. "252 Powerful Words to Avoid Apocalypse at Job Interview",
https://talentculture.com/252-powerful-words-to-avoid-apocalypse-at-job-interview/
39. "STAR Technique Template for Public Servants",
https://assets.ctfassets.net/txbhe1wabmyx/2xGRntr7BoaREfyuOS7UGC/96dcd67d4c04a544f710dd84d3bf9d76/star-technique-template-apolitical.pdf
40. "9 Tricky Interview Questions (and How to Answer Them) ",
https://careersidekick.com/tricky-interview-questions-and-answers/
41. "Sample Answers to "Tell Me About a Time You Failed",
https://careersidekick.com/time-when-you-failed/
42. "13 Behavioral Questions & Tips to Answer Them Like a Pro! ",
https://www.enago.com/academy/behavioral-questions-tips-to-answer-them/

43. "How to Answer Difficult Behavioral Interview Questions Right",
https://business.tutsplus.com/articles/behavioral-interview-questions-and-answers--cms-27647
44. "35 Behavioral Interview Questions — and Strategies for Answering Them",
https://builtin.com/job-interview/behavioral-interview-questions
45. "21+ Behavioral Interview Questions (+Sample Answers) ",
https://novoresume.com/career-blog/behavioral-interview-questions
46. "Answering "Tell Me About A Time You Failed" In A Job Interview [2022] ",
https://www.algrim.co/180-tell-me-about-a-time-you-failed
47. "Leadership Interview Questions & Answers",
https://www.wikijob.co.uk/interview-advice/interview-questions/leadership-interview-questions
48. "How to Answer Interview Questions About Teamwork",
https://www.thebalancecareers.com/how-to-respond-to-interview-questions-about-teamwork-2061100
49. "Common Teamwork Interview Questions and Answers",
https://www.thebalancecareers.com/teamwork-job-interview-questions-and-answers-2064066
50. "Top 35 Teamwork Interview Questions (Example Answers Included) ",
https://theinterviewguys.com/teamwork-interview-questions/
51. "Best Common Teamwork Related Interview Questions and Answers",
https://www.interviewkickstart.com/interview-questions/teamwork-job-interview-questions
52. "Behavioral Interviews",
https://resources.biginterview.com/category/behavioral-interviews/
53. "Answering Behavioral Questions: Problem Solving",
https://resources.biginterview.com/behavioral-interviews/behavioral-interview-question-problem-solving/
54. "What Is Your Greatest Accomplishment? [3 Proven Answers] ",
https://novoresume.com/career-blog/what-is-your-greatest-accomplishment
55. "How to Answer the Interview Question: "What Is Your Greatest Accomplishment?" ",
https://www.wikijob.co.uk/interview-advice/interview-questions/what-is-your-greatest-accomplishment
56. "The Perfect Formula for Answering "What Is Your Greatest Accomplishment" in an Interview",
https://www.themuse.com/advice/greatest-accomplishment-interview-question-answer-examples
57. "Interview Question: "What Is Your Greatest Accomplishment?",
https://www.indeed.com/career-advice/interviewing/what-is-your-greatest-accomplishment
58. "21 Answers to 'What is Your Greatest Accomplishment' Interview Question",
https://futureofworking.com/what-is-your-greatest-accomplishment/
59. "How to Recognize a Strong Work Ethic? ",
https://www.talentlyft.com/en/blog/article/261/how-to-recognize-a-strong-work-ethic
60. "How to Answer "What is Your Greatest Accomplishment?",
https://resources.biginterview.com/behavioral-interviews/greatest-accomplishment-question/
61. "Answering Behavioral Interview Questions: Work Ethic",
https://resources.biginterview.com/behavioral-interviews/work-ethic/

62. "Answering Behavioral Questions: Tell Me About a Time You Failed",
https://resources.biginterview.com/behavioral-interviews/biggest-failure-question/
63. "Answering Leadership Interview Questions",
https://resources.biginterview.com/behavioral-interviews/leadership-interview-questions/
64. "How to Answer Conflict Interview Questions (With Examples) ",
https://resources.biginterview.com/behavioral-interviews/behavioral-interview-questions-conflict/
65. "10 Answers to 'Tell Me a Time You Had a Conflict at Work' Interview Question",
https://futureofworking.com/tell-me-a-time-you-had-a-conflict-at-work/
66. "Conflict Resolution Job Interview Questions",
https://megainterview.com/home/conflict-resolution-interview-questions-answers/
67. "Nonverbal Communication Skills: Definition and Examples",
https://www.indeed.com/career-advice/career-development/nonverbal-communication-skills?from=careeradvice-US
68. "Interview Question: "How Do You Work Under Pressure?",
https://www.indeed.com/career-advice/interviewing/interview-question-how-do-you-work-under-pressure
69. "Answering the "How Do You Work Under Pressure?" Interview Question",
https://www.internships.com/career-advice/interview/how-do-you-work-under-pressure
70. "Interview Question: "How Do You Work Under Pressure?",
https://www.indeed.com/career-advice/interviewing/interview-question-how-do-you-work-under-pressure
71. "Answering 'How Do You Work Under Pressure?' in an Interview",
https://www.glassdoor.com/blog/guide/how-do-you-work-under-pressure/
72. "Tell me about a time when you had to learn something new – 7 sample answers",
https://interviewpenguin.com/tell-me-about-a-time-when-you-had-to-learn-something-new/
73. "Job Interview Questions About Adaptability",
https://megainterview.com/home/job-interview-questions-about-adaptability-answers/
74. "Adaptability interview questions and answers",
https://resources.workable.com/adaptability-interview-questions
75. "Communication Job Interview Questions & Answers",
https://megainterview.com/home/communication-job-interview-questions-answers/
76. "Communication Skills Interview Questions",
https://www.best-job-interview.com/communication-skills-interview-questions.html
77. "Interview Question: "How Do You Handle Meeting Tight Deadlines?",
https://www.indeed.com/career-advice/interviewing/handle-tight-deadlines-interview-question
78. "Time Management & Prioritization Job Interview Questions",
https://megainterview.com/home/time-management-prioritization-interview-questions-answers/
79. "How to Answer Interview Questions About Time Management",
https://www.thebalancecareers.com/time-management-interview-questions-2061286
80. "How To Develop A Creative Approach to Problem Solving",
https://everydayinterviewtips.com/how-to-develop-a-creative-approach-to-problem-solving/
81. "7 Behavioral Interview Questions About Your Creative Thinking Skills",
https://everydayinterviewtips.com/7-behavioural-interview-questions-about-your-creative-thinking-skills-2/

82. "Creative Thinking Job Interview Questions",
https://megainterview.com/home/creative-thinking-job-interview-questions-answers/
83. "What Is Creative Thinking? ",
https://www.thebalancecareers.com/creative-thinking-definition-with-examples-2063744
84. "Attention to Detail Interview Questions",
https://snaphunt.com/resources/sourcing-and-assessing-talent/attention-to-detail-interview-questions
85. "12 Detail Oriented Interview Questions (With Example Answers) ",
https://www.indeed.com/career-advice/interviewing/detail-oriented-interview-questions
86. "How to Answer Detail-Oriented Interview Questions",
https://www.glassdoor.com/blog/guide/detail-oriented/
87. "How to Dress for a Job Interview",
https://www.thebalancecareers.com/how-to-dress-for-an-interview-2061163
88. "Best Questions to Ask an Interviewer",
https://www.thebalancecareers.com/questions-to-ask-in-a-job-interview-2061205
89. "What Are Behavioral Interview Questions and How Do You Write Them? ",
https://www.cedrsolutions.com/behavioral-interview-questions/
90. "65+ Best Questions to Ask an Interviewer & Land Top Jobs",
https://zety.com/blog/questions-to-ask-an-interviewer
91. "57 Smart Questions to Ask in a Job Interview in 2022",
https://www.themuse.com/advice/51-interview-questions-you-should-be-asking
92. "Questions Not to Ask an Employer During a Job Interview",
https://www.thebalancecareers.com/questions-not-to-ask-an-employer-during-a-job-interview-2061107
93. "Zoom Interview Tips: Background, Attire & More",
https://zety.com/blog/zoom-interview-tips
94. "Video interview",
https://resume.io/blog/video-interview
95. "Video Interview Tips: A Job Candidate's Checklist",
https://www.roberthalf.com/blog/job-interview-tips/screen-time-how-to-nail-your-next-video-interview
96. "Video Interview Guide: Tips for a Successful Interview",
https://www.indeed.com/career-advice/interviewing/video-interview-guide
97. "20 Video Interview Tips to Help You Dazzle the Hiring Manager and Get the Job",
https://www.themuse.com/advice/video-interview-tips
98. "How to Ace an Online Job Interview",
https://www.wired.com/story/tips-for-online-job-interviews/
99. "Video interview tips - 11 ways to impress the hiring manager",
https://www.hays.net.nz/career-advice/interview-tips/video-interview-tips
100. "How To Create a STAR Method Resume (With Examples) ",
https://www.indeed.com/career-advice/resumes-cover-letters/star-method-resume
101. "Using the STAR Method to Create a Superior Resume (Examples) ",
https://www.zipjob.com/blog/star-method-resume/
102. "How to Write a STAR Method Resume (with Examples) ",
https://resumegenius.com/blog/resume-help/star-method-resume
103. "How to Create a STAR Method Resume (With Examples) ",
https://himalayas.app/advice/star-method-resume

104. "Writing Strong Resume Bullets",
https://coller.tau.ac.il/sites/nihul_en.tau.ac.il/files/media_server/Recanati/management/IMBA/Career/2016-17/3.%20Writing%20Strong%20Resume%20Bullets_2016_Final.pdf

105. "How to Write the Perfect Resume - STAR Competency based CV",
https://www.linkedin.com/pulse/20140407100337-2150229-how-to-write-a-resume-i-enjoy-reading

106. "How To Use The S.T.A.R Method To Write A Cover Letter",
https://www.teachingcove.com/writing/how-to-write-a-cover-letter/

107. "The Cover Letter",
https://www.amherst.edu/system/files/media/Cover%2520letter%2520guide%2520Redesign.pdf

108. "Maximizing Your Cover Letter",
https://your.yale.edu/sites/default/files/maximizing_your_coverletter_guide_2016.pdf

109. "5 tips to write a rock star cover letter",
https://www2.deloitte.com/ca/en/pages/careers/articles/5-steps-to-a-rock-star-cover-letter.html

110. "How to write a cover letter",
https://nationalcareers.service.gov.uk/careers-advice/covering-letter

111. "What To Do After an Interview: 9 Tips to Help You Succeed",
https://www.indeed.com/career-advice/interviewing/what-to-do-after-an-interview

112. "Follow-Up Email Examples For After the Interview",
https://www.indeed.com/career-advice/interviewing/follow-up-email-examples-after-interview

113. "Tips for Following Up After a Job Interview",
https://www.thebalancecareers.com/how-to-follow-up-after-a-job-interview-2061333

114. "How do I follow up after an interview? Use these 3 examples to help",
https://www.betterup.com/blog/how-to-follow-up-after-an-interview

115. "10 Common Job Interview Mistakes (and How to Avoid Them) ",
https://www.job-hunt.org/avoid-interview-mistakes/

116. "How to Leverage Body Language in Job Interviews",
https://www.job-hunt.org/interview-body-language/

117. "Common Interview Mistakes and What To Do Instead",
https://www.indeed.com/career-advice/interviewing/job-interview-mistakes

118. "How to Show Your Personality at a Job Interview",
https://www.thebalancecareers.com/how-to-show-your-personality-at-an-interview-2061310

119. "How to Get Your Personality Across in Interviews",
https://firsthand.co/blogs/interviewing/how-to-get-your-personality-across-in-interviews

120. "How to show your personality in a job interview",
https://megainterview.com/how-to-show-your-personality-in-an-interview/

121. "7 interview skills that will get you hired in 2022",
https://resume.io/blog/interview-skills-hired

122. "8 Body Language Tips for Your Next Job Interview (Because It's Just as Important as What You Say) ",
https://www.themuse.com/advice/interview-body-language-tips

123. "18 Body Language Tips To Remember During Your Next Interview",
https://www.indeed.com/career-advice/interviewing/body-language-during-interview

124. "Body Language Tips for Your Next Job Interview",
https://www.thebalancecareers.com/body-language-tips-for-your-next-job-interview-2060576
125. "21 job interview questions that are designed to trick you",
https://www.theladders.com/career-advice/21-job-interview-questions-designed-to-trick-you
126. "The Best Way To Answer Teamwork Interview Questions",
https://resources.biginterview.com/behavioral-interviews/teamwork-interview-questions/

Made in the USA
Las Vegas, NV
23 October 2023

79580582R00083